Table of Contents

My Invisible Disability

Published by
Adonis & Abbey Publishers Ltd
P.O. Box 43418
London
SE11 4XZ
http://www.adonis-abbey.com

First Edition, January 2006

British Library Cataloguing-in-Publication Data
A catalogue record for this book is available from the British Library

ISBN 1-905068-25-5

Cover Design   Mega Graphix

Tonja you giving me a place to live is where my story began, Even though out west was tough it brought me to where I am today. I am grateful for the help you, your dad and family gave me.

Love) [signature] Ephs 4:1

My Invisible Disability

By

Greg Noack

Adonis & Abbey
Publishers Ltd

Dedication

For Mom, Bob, and the forgotten; and to those who did not forget, thank you.

Prologue

On November tenth, nineteen ninety-six my life changed forever. Writing about the event that occurred on that day allowed me to heal. It took almost seven years to write my story, and whenever I wrote, I benefited emotionally and psychologically from expressing my feelings regarding this traumatic story that is my story.

I owe much to John Tudor, my social worker, who suggested writing to help cope with the many emotions and thoughts that ran through my injured brain. Instead of being "pumped" full of medication, I wrote to become better. I especially took his advice after being on antidepressants for one month. During this time, I really thought there was something wrong with me. Consequently, I stopped the medication of my own accord and took up the pen. However, I will not say that antidepressants did not help me. Such medication regenerated chemicals and processes that were absent owing to my traumatic brain injury. These drugs simply were not the whole answer for me, what I needed most to come to grips with the changes that took place in my life.

As I continued to write my story, I realized the wonderful love of God and the power of faith. Without God, I would not be here or even capable of writing. He gave His Son for me, and by doing so He gave me a chance at eternity, but most importantly as regards this book, however, He saved me that night to believe so.

By keeping a journal of my experiences over the past seven years, I also realized the incredible level of ignorance that the so-called normal members of the population display towards mental disability, the physically disabled, and the elderly. The love that such people showed me should not be ignored when it is offered to anyone, but received graciously and returned.

Today's vain society is too quick to look at appearance and beauty, make inane judgments and overlook inner beauty. Hopefully, my story will enlighten you and introduce you to such forgotten people of society. Because, as the saying goes, the best cure for ignorance of this variety is knowledge.

"And we rejoice in the hope of the glory of God. Not only so, but we also rejoice in our sufferings, because we know that suffering produces perseverance; perseverance, character; and character, hope. And hope does not disappoint us, because God has poured out His love into our hearts by the Holy Spirit, whom He has given us."
Romans 5:2-5 (King James Version)

Foreword

It is estimated that close to 2 million people suffer head injuries every year in North America alone. From concussions- the mildest form of head injury- to severe trauma the numbers are staggering. And most of them are preventable.

"Brain injury". The term elicits catastrophic images of disability, dependency and a life of helpless struggle.

Or does it?

While nobody can deny the difficulties of living with such a problem, the fact is that with adequate treatment and support, patients who survive a brain injury can and do live productive fulfilling lives.

Greg Noack is a true example of such cases.

I met Greg at the Toronto Rehabilitation Institute, Neurorehabilitation program, not as a patient but as a team member and colleague.

That fact alone speaks volumes about his determination and inner strength. As the reader will find out, Greg has "been there" and back. He suffered a catastrophic injury that altered his life, destroyed his former self and made him confront his deepest fears.

Greg understands the process of recovery. The pain, anxiety and the uncertainty that such injuries cause. Therein lays his strength.

Greg is a true survivor, and he has been kind and generous enough to let us into his world and share his experiences. The good ones and the bad ones. The times when he was vulnerable; when life as he knew it ceased to be.

We learn about love, family and friends. About treatment team members and hospitals. We learn about anger, sadness and frustration. Yet overall the theme that permeates this book is courage. Courage to persevere and never give up.

To disclose the "unmentionables" and be comfortable with it. Courage to be a care giver to those who like him, have been injured; who suffer from the same tribulations Greg did.

It would be much easier to work in other endeavours, removed from hospitals, rehabilitation and care-giving. But as the reader will learn, it is not Greg's style. And we all benefit from it.

A. Snaiderman, M.D, F.R.C.P(C).
Director, Neuropsychiatry Clinic,
Neurorehabilitation Program.
Toronto Rehabilitation Institute.
Dept. of Psychiatry, University of Toronto.

Chapter 1

Up To That Point

I looked down to the auditorium floor between my feet. I could see the silhouette of my upper body and head but not a clear reflection. The floor was shiny but scuffed by the plastic chairs used for many occasions and the sporting events held here. I continued to stare for a while. The speaker/teacher was reading out last names beginning with K and granting them diplomas; I was an N, so I would be called soon. I was lost in my thoughts as I looked down at my shadow on the floor.

I do not know if it was the roast beef dinner prepared by the culinary students, the humidity of the gymnasium, or my nerves. It was probably all of the above with an asterisk beside nerves for emphasis. I began to think, or perhaps the better way to say it would be to say that I began to question what I was to do once this ceremony was over. Is this what I really wanted? I failed my first year of university and thought that I'd better try college and get my marketing diploma. What other choice did I have? Upgrade my high school? Maybe business was not for me, I thought, and I had overlooked the subtle hint of that truth that failure at university should have been for me. I blamed that failure on independence, on being nineteen and away from home for the first time, with no father dictating what I should do and how to do it. I preferred beer and pizza to books and tests.

I was starting to get scared about going out into the working world without the protection of school. I complained about this place while I went, but now it seemed like I wished I could be back in my first year. I had to accept the fact that I could not turn back time and that I was getting older. The expectations I held for myself had to be fulfilled with the passing of time, but before too much time had passed. By twenty-five, I hoped to have a wife, to be thinking about starting a family, and have a home — the "picket fence" thing.

I quietly belched into my fist and quickly lifted up my head. I had brought up some of my dinner and hoped that it was first year students who prepared this decadent meal and not graduates, because they still seemed to have much to learn. I took a drink while waiting to start my walk up to accept the pieces of paper that gave purpose to my life for the past three years, four if you counted the fun at university.

"Along with his Business Administration Marketing Diploma and Human Resources Certificate, Greg Noack is also the recipient of the Student Leadership Award."

"Hmmm," I muttered to myself as I stood up and made my way through the maze of people sitting at their tables. I was surprised by the award, and proud of myself, I think. I climbed the four stairs to the stage and shook the speaker's hand.

"Thank you."

"Congratulations, Greg, and good luck."

I turned away and began my walk back to my seat with a smattering of applause echoing in the large auditorium, mostly Mom and the people at my table. While walking I was perplexed by two things, the good luck comment by the speaker and the unexpected leadership award. What had I led myself into?

Choices

I graduated from college in 1995 at the age of twenty-three and set out to find a job in Windsor, Ontario. Unlike the majority of my classmates, I decided not to go on to university and get my bachelor's degree for business in the fall. I took my chances in the competitive job market with a diploma but no degree, a chance that did not pay off. This was yet another key decision I made in my life that backfired.

When the leaves on the trees started to change colour, I was still without work. I was becoming frustrated but continued to beat the pavement for work. My persistence finally paid off, however, and after a series of interviews, I became the manager in training for a discount department store. But my satisfaction would quickly turn to anger, stress, and frustration.

The three months of training to become a manager were like boot camp. Hour-long commutes to different stores and unloading freight made me question the title of manager. I did become a manager eventually, but it was short-lived because three months was all I could take. My salary was 28,500 Canadian dollars per year. When I signed my contract, it seemed like a large amount for the forty-five to fifty hours a week I expected, but it was not enough for the seventy to eighty hours I actually worked.

After quitting, I doubted my quick departure as I was back in the job market with my working ability in question. Explaining why I had left this job after six months was a hindrance and even seemed to ruin my chances of getting other work as future employers made sure to question that fact and to point out that I was only a manager for three months.

"So Greg, why did you leave?" a prospective employer would ask.

"Because they worked my butt off and treated me like crap" is how I wanted to answer, but instead I would reply, "Lack of upper management support."

The interviewer then would wince and show me the door, which was something I would grow accustomed to over the next three months. In my four years of post secondary schooling, I was never taught how to respond to such a question. The college, I assume, did not want to give the impression that you could fail when you graduate.

Job opportunities were not the only things I was having difficulty finding. My girl hunting, in chauvinistic terms, was at a low point. It had been three years since my last serious relationship. Though this was on my mind, employment was still my major concern. Not having a paycheck did not allow for too many dinners, movies, and gifts. So a good job was something I thought was essential to finding a partner in life.

In spite of this lack of success, however, my life after graduation was starting to pick up speed somewhat like an avalanche. Time was moving very fast and I was swept up in it. Minutes were like seconds, hours like minutes, weeks like days, and months like weeks. The end of June rolled around, and still I had no direction in my life. My mother, on the other hand, did. She had re-established a connection with her high school sweetheart and got married in May. I guess the third time was a charm as Brian was my mother's third husband.

Brian is a wonderful, caring man whom my mother certainly deserved. The only drawback was that he lived in British Columbia. My mother had planned to move out West at the end of October, and through her plans, I derived one as well. Since I was having no luck with the job market and relationship department, why not go out West myself?

Brian has two sons and two daughters close to my age. I had met his one daughter, Tonja, three previous times. She was nice, and through discussions with her, offered to give me a place to live until I got settled. With the money I stashed away from managing, I purchased a mountain bike and a plane ticket to Vancouver. I also had enough funds to live for a few months. My plan was set and my plane left on June 28, five days before my twenty-fourth birthday.

I left quickly and without much fanfare. I said goodbye to my family and really had no close friends to bid farewell. I liked leaving without notice because I did not care for the people, particularly my so-called friends, who were in my life.

I was a loner, and consequently getting a country's distance between myself, and the life I was living, was another benefit to the decision to move out West. I thought that when I made it big all those so-called friends would be even more impressed that I had the courage to jump on a plane and start anew, making it on my own, without them.

I got off the plane with my belongings in tow. I would send for my bike later. I was quite scared and nervous being in a place that was large and new to me. Bus rides and a ferry (boat) finally brought me to my destination: Victoria, British Columbia.

The beauty of Vancouver Island amazed me. The snow-covered mountains, the large trees, and the ocean views were all breathtaking. I was excited about my new surroundings and wanted to settle in this beautiful place. I had heard of BC's beauty, and the rumour spreading in Ontario was that it was more employee-friendly with respect to finding work. I rolled up my sleeves and started to pound the pavement. I wanted to find work quickly because I did not want to impose on my stepsister for too long. Making her seven-year old son sleep on the couch and residing in his room made me feel like a first-class heel.

I had hoped that coming out here might have slowed me down, or more specifically, slowed the passing of time. The twenty-five year age limit was coming up quickly, leaving me just a year to fulfill the aspirations I had tied to that point in my life. Everything would slow down once I got work, or so I hoped.

Same candy, different wrapper

My other stepsister, Sharlene, who worked at the University of Victoria, got me a few shifts of envelope stuffing for conventions held at the University. In the two months I was in Victoria that was all I could get in the way of employment. The rumour that spread back East was definitely false, as the job prospects were slim at best.

Victoria is a government town without "Big Industry" to compare to the Big Three automakers found in southern Ontario. Tourism is the reason that such industry has not been invited here, to keep the beauty of the countryside intact. But the beauty of it all was wearing thin. If one more employer asked me why I left managing so quickly I was going to staple their tie or blouse to their desk and say, "Because of my warm, sparkling personality, that's why they friggin' canned me."

I was at the point of removing my managerial experience from my résumé but decided not to. If I had a year of nothingness on my résumé, I was sure that fact would be questioned just as much and would leave the impression I was one picky employee. I did receive good news regarding finding a place to live however. I did not want to wear out my welcome with Tonja and found out that one of my college friends back in Windsor, Allison, wanted to give BC a try too. Because the rent was so high, we decided to live together. It also meant I would have to take a less-than-great job in another field, the service industry.

As of September 1, I was living in a two-bedroom, one-and-half bathroom rented condo with a fireplace, indoor pool, tennis court and view of the water, the Gorge inlet. I also landed a job as a night cleaner for a cleaning company who contracted out work to five-star restaurants and hotels. The job paid for my rent and living expenses but nothing more. To say I was happy with how things were going would be a large overstatement.

Simple wants

I awoke from my three-hour sleep and looked up at the dark ceiling in my bedroom. I slept on a futon mattress placed on the floor. I used a milk crate turned on its side as my nightstand. I could not afford furnishings on what I made, and I used what little money I had stashed away from managing to eat. You can't eat furniture.

I looked at my alarm clock that read ten o'clock; I had to be at the five-star restaurant and hotel by eleven. My shifts were Friday, Saturday, Sunday and Monday from eleven at night to six in the morning. Being a newcomer, I received the shifts that no one else wanted. It made for an entertaining weekend.

Before I arose from my mattress, I looked around my bare room. The floor was covered with crumpled old newspapers that I had scoured for jobs. I looked like one of the street people lying on the sidewalk downtown. The sad thing was that I felt that way. I stared up at the dark ceiling once again and said, "Give me a sign damn it! Is this it? Is this what my life is going to be?"

I was talking at, and making demands of, God — not praying to Him. I had some nerve to talk that way to Him considering I did nothing for my relationship with Him. A Lutheran Church confirmed me in my hometown of Sault Ste. Marie, Ontario when I was thirteen years old. I guess I thought confirmed meant I did not have to go to church, because the only time since my confirmation that I went to church was for a wedding or funeral.

I actually expected to see something in the darkness of my room, but of course I did not.

"Just as I thought," I said, opening the door to my room and entering the bathroom to shower. Like everything else, my relationship with God was a matter of blame and frustration, as both my employment situation and relationship status were

17

going nowhere.

I quickly showered as I had to be on the ten forty bus. I usually rode my bike, but the past week I had to resort to the transit system and the "shoe lace express." I had broken my back brakes in a fit of anger as I tried to repair them a couple of weeks earlier and could not afford to pay for the damage I created. Allison offered her bike but made sure to comment about the batteries running low in her light, so I thought, why bother.

I did not mind the long walk home after work anyway and started to get used to it. I had to because the buses did not run until seven in the morning. My co-workers would tell me I walked and lived in a rough area, but I did not hesitate to walk home because it was so beautiful. Compared to the places back East where I lived, this was paradise.

I threw on my green work jeans, blue work shirt, green fleece pullover, maroon denim jacket and grabbed my toque and gloves. It was early November and getting cold at four in the morning. I grabbed a five-dollar bill and left my wallet in the bathroom. I never carried it just in case I did run into trouble. I really did not have to worry anyway because I was broke.

"Greg, why don't you take my bike?" Allison asked.

She did not mention the light for a change.

"Na, screw it. I don't mind the walk. It lets me think." Which was something that I did too much.

My roommate and I were on better terms. We had gotten into a big argument two weeks earlier but were getting closer and at least tolerable to one another. Living together had put a strain on our friendship.

"Okay, see ya tomorrow morning. Be careful."

"Yeah, see ya." As I turned and walked out the door, I mumbled, "I think I am going to jump off that bridge on my way home tonight." I was referring to a bridge on our street above a bicycle trail and creek.

As I locked the door I heard Allison ask, "What did you say?" I did not respond as I went down the elevator.

I waited for the bus and contemplated my life to that moment. What was I doing and how the heck was I going to ever make it given what I was doing. The bus doors opened and I dropped my coins in for the fare. The bus jerked forward as it started again. I looked out the window into the darkness as I sat, seeing only my reflection in the glass.

"Loser." I said to myself.

After a twenty-minute walk, I opened the door to the lavish hotel I worked at. What people paid for the night is what I made in two shifts of cleaning up after them. My job consisted of cleaning four bathrooms, the kitchen, and the restaurant located in this five-star hotel, as well as the hotel's lobby. I wanted to work faster that night because my beloved Forty-Niners were on at ten in the morning and I did not want to sleep through the game, damn Western three-hour time change.

I am a huge fan of American football. Canadian football with its gigantic end zones annoyed me. Didn't they understand that having small end zones made it harder to score and added to the excitement of the game? The championship game always produced an excellent game, however.

My angry mood was not subsiding but starting to erupt as my shift went on. Cleaning toilet bowls and tampon dispensers was not why I went to school for three years. It was approaching three-thirty and I wanted to start my trek home by four-thirty. I would then be home by six, sleep for four hours, and get up to watch the game.

"This sucks. Why am I doing this?" I said to Colin, my co-worker.

We were having a soda at the bar in the restaurant that

overlooked the beautiful inner harbour of Victoria. He did not have an answer and shrugged his shoulders. I envied Colin. He too was from back East. He was four years younger than me and enjoyed getting by on what he made cleaning. He did not get stressed about things like I did.

"Well Greg, maybe things will improve with that new job that you are starting on Tuesday."

I was recently hired by a respected department store in the menswear department. It was temporary part-time work for the Holiday season. I would only receive up to eighteen hours a week, so I would have to keep a couple shifts of cleaning.

"Yeah, I am looking forward to measuring men's inseams and telling people, 'No, we don't have anymore extra boxes!'"

We chuckled, finished our sodas, got up, and went our separate ways.

"See ya tomorrow," I said as I put on my gloves and hat.

"Ya, you too," Colin responded.

We both turned and went in opposite directions. It was an extremely foggy night, and when I turned to look back for Colin, he was already out of sight.

My walk consisted of about forty-five minutes through downtown and then another forty-five on the main street I lived on. I did not mind it because the city was so surreal, and this night it was especially surreal as the fog rolled in over the harbour and into the downtown corridors. I stopped at my usual café where I would buy a coffee and stay drinking it as the night turned to day. I glanced at the clock and it read four-twenty.

"I'll have a large double, double and a raisin bagel --- to go," I said to the coffee server.

The server had just wiped the chalkboard calendar above the cash register clean and wrote a ten beneath November. Another day in my life wiped away, I thought to myself, as I decided not to stay because I wanted to be home in time to sleep and get up and watch the football game. I gave him the five and got six cents in change. It was not exactly cheap, but after a hard shift of cleaning other people's filth, I deserved it.

I came to the street that I lived on. I was halfway home. I walked for ten minutes and came to another coffee shop. I took off my glove and checked my pocket. I only had six cents, which I should have remembered, but I was getting tired. I continued to walk and came to the bridge on my street. The idea of jumping was in my thoughts, but this time they were muted, as I felt extremely weak. I would never jump anyway because of the pain it would cause my family, especially my mother.

I took my hand out of my pocket. It seemed like I had my hand in there for some time. God I was tired. I do not know what came over me, but I was so exhausted that, after I took my hand out of my pocket, I decided to lay down right on the sidewalk. As I lowered my head to the pebbly cement and slowly turned over onto my back, I noticed that I was not on the same side of the street I was on when I first checked my pocket for money for a coffee.

Chapter 2

The Sign

"Hello."

"Is Greg in?" My sister Kim was calling from Windsor to say hi. Kim is the kind of person who worries, who loves and cares for her family dearly, to the point that, when I lived in Windsor and jogged to her house and then back, I would have to call her when I got home.

"No he isn't. He isn't back from work yet, which is strange. Have you heard from him?" Allison mistook Kim for my stepsister, Tonja, which made Kim panic.

"This is his sister Kim, from Windsor. Why would I have heard from him?"

"Oh, Kim. I thought you were Tonja."

"Where is Greg? Is everything all right?"

Allison explained to Kim how I planned to walk home from work last night and was home usually at around six or seven. Kim started to panic and told Allison to call her when I got in. Kim started to voice her concerns to my brother, my other sister, and father, all of who lived in Ontario. She also talked to my mother, who already knew something was up from talking to Allison and was on her way to Victoria from the mainland.

"Victoria Police Department."

"Hello, my name is Allison, and I am concerned about my roommate."

"Has he been missing for more than twenty-four hours?"

"No, he has not. But he is usually home from his job by six or seven in the morning, and it is ten o'clock."

"Maybe he is at a friend's." The dispatcher had taken hundreds of these calls before, but this conversation with Allison seemed to have her attention, in spite of her stock answers.

"He is fairly new to Victoria and does not have any real close friends out here. Plus, he would call me and let me know."

"What about family?"

"He has step-family, but I have already contacted them." With all the questions the dispatcher was asking, Allison started to realize that something was up. The police did not usually show concern until a day passed.

"Can you give a description of your roommate and tell me where he worked."

"He is about five eight, slim but built, and weighs about one hundred and seventy pounds. He was wearing green jeans, a burgundy denim jacket over a green fleece pullover, and his blue work shirt. He was also wearing gloves and a hat."

"Where does he work?"

"He works as a janitor at one of the fancy hotels downtown."

"Okay. We will get back to you if something comes up, and if twenty-four hours goes by without hearing from him, we will file a missing person's report."

After giving the dispatcher our phone number, Allison waited. The reason they took Allison's concerns seriously was that they had discovered a body on the Gorge Bridge earlier that morning that fitted my description. Allison's exact description was important because that body was I and my means of identification, which was in my wallet, was on the toilet tank in my bathroom.

I was taken to the Royal Jubilee Hospital with severe head injuries and a small laceration over my left eye. I was unconscious and once examined by the doctors at that hospital, I was transferred to Victoria General Hospital's neurological ward. I had fallen into a coma.

"Hello Allison, this is the Victoria Police. Does your roommate have any photo identification?"

"As a matter of fact, his wallet, which contains his driver's license, is here."

"Okay, we will send over some officers."

Within minutes, Allison gave my ID to the police, and they identified me as the victim of an assault that could ultimately be a homicide. They returned with my identification and broke the news to Allison. As the officer handed my wallet to Allison, he said, "Allison, did Greg know anyone near the Gorge Road Bridge?"

Allison knew that bridge because it was located just down our street, and the last thing she heard from me was that I was going to jump from it. She began to weep uncontrollably, thinking I had taken my own life.

"No, no he is okay. He was beaten up pretty badly and was found on that bridge," the officer said.

Allison was able to compose herself and was relieved that I was alive and did not take my own life. She then took down what hospital I was at and contacted my family and friends. She was quite calm for the situation she was in. Because I had said those stupid things the previous night, and without knowing how severely beaten I was, she found the mere fact that I was alive a calming influence.

She waited for my mother, who was on her way from the mainland as soon as Allison stated that I was not home that morning. When she arrived, she and Allison and my stepfather, Brian, went to the hospital, not knowing what to expect. The only thing they knew was that I was alive. My family back East were also worried by what could have happened to their brother and son.

I had made things difficult for everyone, even the police, as I had left my wallet at home. I had left it there for this very reason, so that I could not be robbed, but then I never thought this would happen. Even if I did have my wallet on me, all I had in it was a driver's license. I had no credit cards. If only I had seen this coming. All I ever wanted was a girlfriend and a good job. That is why I came out West. Maybe that was asking for too much, and maybe I had not realized what I already had and now could lose.

Is this it?

A jack-o-lantern with plums for eyes is how my mother would later describe what she seen when she entered my hospital room with my stepfather and roommate. I was so badly beaten around the head and neck area that the swelling resulted in this grotesque appearance.

I received a severe blow to the back right side of my head that was so vicious that the frontal lobes of my brain were damaged from the force. The power of the blow caused my brain to move forward and strike the front of my skull and then bounce to the back again before it settled into its original position. In medical terms, coup-contra-coup is the name for such movement of the brain. The doctors determined that this enormous blow had left me unconscious and, along with the kicks and punches to my head, caused my comatose state.

The police found a large splinter of wood covered with my blood on the bridge, just a few inches from my body. The assumption could be made the initial severe blow was caused by a baseball bat or other blunt object. The welts and wounds around my eyes and ears were from kicking and stomping. My neck also showed welts and bruising and gave the indication of strangulation. To the amazement of the police as well as the doctors, I received no other injuries except a large bruise across the front of my chest. However, my brain had received such trauma that it was essentially jolted out of order and needed rest to reset itself. The question was whether my brain would turn on again, and if it did, could it remember how to start everything and function normally.

An intravenous (IV) line was placed in my arm and on my toe was a clip, similar to a clothes peg, measuring my pulse and blood oxygen saturation. A Nasal-Gastric (NG) tube was pushed up my nose and a condom catheter was placed over my penis instead of a normal catheter because I was pulling things out of myself. I was also in a diaper because I could not control such functions, my brain obviously not sending or receiving the appropriate signals, and even if it were, I could not exactly get up while in a coma. The CAT scan and MRI revealed that my basic brain architecture was okay, but there was much concern about what was causing my deterioration. The brain is so complex that even the most expert doctors in the field of brain research do not know what to expect in terms of recovery. After a week had gone by, I was still comatose but showed signs of waking up. All I remember from that week of my life was gagging and choking and hearing the nurses converse, saying things like, "We almost got it," as they reset my NG tube because I had pulled it out.

My father made the trip and did not handle the situation well. Fear and paranoia overwhelmed him, and he and his fiancée Cathy had to leave at one point to change hotels. After he saw the effects of the brutality done to his son, hotels without proper locks on the windows simply would not do. He also got my roommate to photocopy the crime bulletin in the newspaper for he feared that if someone saw him making copies of it they would link him to me and attack him also.

He stayed for six days and left on the tenth day of my coma. I started to fall back into dire straits after he left, and maybe it was good that he did not stay because I was near death and his tendency was to yell at me, expecting responses as if all he had to do was speak more loudly to get through, and hold me still so I would not pull any IVs out again. In fact, apparently I did respond to questions after a dramatic hesitation, and I would answer correctly, but now I cannot remember being asked or answering.

The stimulation my father was causing was not good for my recovery. My mother was advised not even to pat my arm gently, because my brain could not equate what such a small thing like caressing meant, and it would cause unhealthy confusion.

On the thirteenth day, a metal rod was inserted into my skull. It was inserted to measure the intracranial pressure in my brain, pressure caused by the swelling of the brain itself. My resting heart rate fluctuated to one hundred and eighty, and with that symptom, I was put back into intensive care. The doctors were extremely concerned and did more tests, now worried that there may have been damage to the stem of my brain.

The brainstem controls such things as breathing, and if the oxygen to my brain was being diminished, it could result in retardation or even death. On the fourteenth day since my assault, my brother and two sisters came out to be by my side, to be there for the final moments of my life. My mother was given the talk any parent feared, that I might be severely handicapped, mentally and physically, and that I might die.

The second week of my coma was coming to an end. I was becoming cold to the touch and atrophy was setting in. My arms were curled up so tightly into my chest that my mother could not straighten them. All the muscle mass I had built up over the previous five years wilted away due to my lack of mobility, and whatever calories I was given intravenously were burned up quicker than they could be replaced. I was emaciated and the stalky, hundred and seventy-pound man who had entered this hospital was now one hundred and thirty pounds.

When I was nineteen, I was overweight and weighed two

hundred and twenty pounds. It took me five years of hard work to lose fifty pounds. I lost the weight in a vain attempt to attract women, and now I had lost forty more in just fourteen days.

My brother Scott, sisters Kim and Melissa, mother, stepfather, and roommate sat around me like a campfire. They maintained an unnatural silence, knowing that any noise would cause me harm. The silence was broken when my mother turned to my stepfather and said, in a voice muffled from crying, "Parents are supposed to die first."

With that, my hospital room cleared as the strong emotions finally broke down those gathered around me and they did not want to create any noise. It was now just me left alone in the room and surrounded by machines that kept me going. Maybe it was good I was now alone, because this was my fight and no one else's. This was it, the final struggle.

Answer to prayers

"This cannot be happening. I do not know what I will do if he passes. I just want to get the animals who did this to him and do the same to them." My mother was speaking of revenge to my stepfather. In the conversation outside my room, thoughts of revenge were now setting in along with the very real possibility of me dying.

"I say we stake out that f---ing bridge," my older brother angrily replied.

"Don't be stupid, Scott. Do you want to end up in here too?" My younger sister Melissa was the voice of reason.

"Well, I am going outside for a smoke," Scott said as his bottom lip started to quiver.

"Diane, let's go for a walk. Kim, Allison, and Melissa, you stay here in case something happens," Brian said.

My stepfather has a strong faith in God, and as he and my

mother walked, he turned to her and said, "Diane, do not take this upon yourself. Give it to God. Pray for His help. If it is His will to take Greg now, so be it; but do not take this unto yourself. Only He can take on this burden, and that is what He is there for."

My mother and Brian stopped walking and hugged each other. As they hugged, my mother closed her eyes and set her head on Brian's chest. She said a prayer and gave my situation to God. After the prayer, calm came over my mother. She was no longer taking sole responsibility for whatever happened. She gave it to God as Brian had.

In fact, I received prayers from people I had never expected would pray for me, from the students at my younger sister's high school to my brother-in-law's mother and her Mennonite church. My good friend Denise, who is Native Canadian and attending law school in Toronto, burned tobacco, the smoke carrying her prayer to the Creator, for my recovery. Word of my ordeal had spread throughout my hometown of Sault Ste. Marie, Ontario, and the prayers now came from there too. Prayers came from my best friend Mando, from people in the neighbourhood where I grew up, and even from my grade three public school teacher.

There were also prayers coming from an old flame of mine, and her family who were going through a tough time themselves. Carmen was her name, the first girl with whom I had fallen in love. I met her when I was sixteen and working at my first job. We dated and had our good times together, but our relationship really did not go beyond that. I do not know why the relationship did not develop further, but we still kept in touch eight years later. Carmen's father had a heart attack close to the time I was assaulted, and he was in the hospital for about the same amount of time that I was in a coma. I was coming up on day fifteen of my coma, when, on November 25, Carmen's father lost his battle. As Carmen and her mother drove from the hospital after their tremendous loss, they discussed my situation. They both felt that their father and husband would want me to survive rather than him, because I had my whole life before me.

The clock struck midnight, and with it, the date turned to the twenty-fifth, as it had done three hours earlier back East. I entered day fifteen of my coma, and the people around me, even the doctors, did not know what was in store. A week earlier, I had showed signs of waking, but I now showed signs of dying. People who are in a comatose state show positive signs just before they wake. Any positive indications can reveal that an awakening may soon occur, but I now showed none of these signs.

My siblings and roommate left the hospital and went back to my apartment to get what little rest they could while they waited. However, Mother and Brian stayed just in case the inevitable were to occur. Mom wanted to be by my side if these were to be my final moments.

"I am going to look in on him," my mother said to Brian. Since their walk and talk earlier, Mom seemed more at peace with whatever was going to happen to her son. She started to concentrate her prayers on God taking me and making sure I was okay if I joined Him.

Mom walked in and looked at me, and a smile came over her face. The thoughts of revenge were still there but were somewhat diminished by the assurance that I was in God's hands. Whatever was in store for me, she prayed that He would be there. She walked to my bedside and covered my wired body as much as possible. She had made this walk several times in the past hour. She did not want me to go. Mom was there for me, but these were two weeks that no parent would ever want to go through.

The sad thing was that this was becoming a regular event in beautiful Victoria. On the floor I was on, there were four other victims of violent crimes with severe head trauma. "Curbing" is what they called these vicious attacks. Groups of people would attack an innocent unsuspecting person, and once unconscious, if that person was lucky enough to be unconscious, the victim's mouth was opened and set on the street's curb like they were taking a bite out of it. The back of their head was then kicked, and the victim's teeth caved in with the blow. I was fortunate that my assault never came to that point.

The police linked my attack to a woman's murder on the trail beneath the bridge I was found on and three other assaults in the surrounding area. Because of Victoria's beauty, I naively chose not to heed my fellow worker's warning. That saying "never judge a book by its cover" definitely held for Victoria. It had the second highest number of violent crimes per capita in Canada at the time, which was a fact that I was not aware of.

My mother turned and walked out of my room. As she opened the door, she realized that her son might become a statistic for something she never even imagined in her worst nightmares. She looked back at me once more and went out the door, which slowly closed behind her. Before the door closed completely, she heard something come from my room that she thought she would never hear again.

"Mom."

My belief

God has given us the freedom of deciding whether to be good or evil, and there is a constant battle between Him and the devil to determine which way we go. I had lain unconscious on that sidewalk for approximately one hour between my assault and when I was discovered. This was when the greatest battle of all occurred, my very existence in jeopardy; but more importantly, my eternal existence was in jeopardy too. The fog levitating above me hid what was going on. The conscious mind cannot see or even comprehend such a fight, and this is why such a battle is hidden.

The people who assaulted me, and "curbed" and assaulted others, chose evil and fought for that side. They beat me to within an inch of my life for no reason, and if I passed away, those who did this to me would have succeeded in doing the devil's work. My choice would have been made: I would have never gone to heaven. I never had any relationship with God before my attack, and I had never repented for my wrongdoing. I had sinned, but I never wanted to be accountable. By being sinful and failing to take responsibility, I forfeited my right to eternity in His kingdom. My actions on this earth were not evil, but actions alone do not grant you an afterlife. It is only your core belief that allows you eternity.

I had the opportunity for a relationship with Him but did not get it. Mom and Dad, if he was not sleeping in that day, took us to church every Sunday. I went to Sunday school and carried on with the ritual of church every Sunday until after my confirmation. As I got older, however, I always expected to get something more out of my belief in God, maybe wealth, maybe a girl, something I could hold onto, something tangible, proof that my belief was valid. I thought this reward was the reason to have a relationship with Him, and because I was not receiving anything in return, I wondered why I should put the time and effort into a relationship that is going nowhere. If the battle were lost that day on the bridge, my way of thinking would have left me with only one choice, one destination.

However, God continued to fight for me. He did not turn His back on me, a non-believer you could say. He chose to surround me with the prayers of family and friends because He was not going to let the other side succeed. All the prayers I received — from Denise burning tobacco to my brother in law's Mennonite family's prayer, from my stepfather's faith and his Baptist prayers to Carmen's Catholic faith and the belief that her father's passing was linked to me waking just afterwards — helped me. If not for those prayers, my fight with evil would have been lost.

A majority of these peoples' beliefs may be contrary to my beliefs, but I am not going to deny that their faith had an effect on me waking up. I am not going to judge them and say they are wrong in their beliefs because they are different from mine. Only one being knows what the true story is and in what one should have faith, God Himself.

Before this happened to me, I always wanted proof of God's existence and His love. After my assault, I awakened to suffering; but I was able to persevere because He was helping me, because things happened in my recovery that only can be explained as the presence of God. What I would wake up to and experience is all the proof I need. This is my belief.

Chapter 3

Pot of confusion

"I'll have a large coffee for here please," I said to the person behind the counter. The cafe I was in seemed familiar.

"Here is your cup. Just help yourself," he said while he pointed to the coffee machines.

I looked at the brands on the labels of each machine. The first label was Yukon Dark. The next machine label read Colombian. The third one read CONFUSION. The label was bold and capitalized. What type of flavour is confusion, I thought to myself. I decided to try it. Each machine had a nozzle, which you pulled down to fill your cup. When I lowered it, the cafe erupted like in an explosion similar to one in summer action movies.

"He's awake," my mother said.

Four days would go by until I realized myself that I was awake because I experienced post-traumatic amnesia. Once out of this forgetfulness, I was able to focus on my present surroundings. I awoke to my penis in a condom catheter, and with my mother and Allison, watching the nurse put a new condom on me. This was not a usual catheter because I had earlier developed the habit of pulling out whatever was in me.

The old me would have covered up and been upset, but I was now stripped of those emotions of embarrassment or self-consciousness. I had lost the emotions of laughing and crying too. Fortunately, I had also lost the ability to feel panic, a definite plus. If I had awakened before my incident without the ability to walk or even to move my legs, I do not know how I would have reacted. When I did awaken in that condition after the coma, however, I was calm.

My privacy was lost and I did not care. My manhood was exposed to the world and it did not bother me. I had been very insecure about myself prior to this moment. But now I was in extreme shock. I went from walking home from work to have a night's sleep to this hospital room and the nurse's hands on my penis. I also noticed an IV line in my right arm and a feeding tube up my nose. I had no feeling at all in my legs. It was not that I was paralyzed, but my mind did not know how to direct them. I knew how to move my right arm, however, and I used it to grab things and buzz for the nurses. But the arm moved around chaotically as if it wanted to break away from my body. I could not comprehend what had happened to me. I was startled and confused. Whatever emotions remained available to me, were tossed around like a salad, confusing my injured brain. I went from having a dream to waking up in a hospital bed with a diaper on. Whoever did this to me had put me in a situation where I could lose who I was. I had awakened to a different world, to a different me.

"I'm thirsty," I pleaded.

"Sorry Greg. We are not allowed to give you anything," my mother said pitifully.

I was not allowed liquids for fear of aspirating the liquid, which could then gather in my lungs causing pneumonia. I had dysphasia, which means that I had forgotten how to swallow, and liquid could go down the "wrong tube." Between my thirst, waking up to my new surroundings, and not knowing what had happened to me, I was anxious and irritable. I was in such a traumatic situation, however, that all my mixed up feelings overloaded my brain and resulted in a straight face that revealed nothing.

Even though I was in the fight for my life, the only thing that concerned me at that moment was getting a drink. I tore the IV in my right arm out with my teeth and began sucking the liquid. The nurses and my family were quick to notice and corrected the situation by putting the IV in my left arm and watching over me even closer. They made sure that I could not lift my arm up and do it again.

"I have a headache," I whined.

I did not have one but expected that the nurse would bring me aspirin with a cup of water. I was determined to get my drink.

"Here you go. Open wide," the nurse spoke.

Instead of water, I received a spoonful of vanilla pudding with crushed aspirin mixed in. Whatever taste sensation I had lost could not hide the strong bitter taste of crushed aspirin.

"More please," I said after receiving my tainted dessert.

I just wanted to get rid of the crushed aspirin taste, not get more of the wonderful pudding. I would get used to pudding and applesauce, however, as they were used to wash down my medication. I also learned not to lie about having a headache. My mind knew that the only way to get a drink was to plead to my family. It was so weird. I could have gotten my own water but did not know how to walk. Even so, I probably would not have known how to turn the tap on. Weird still bests described what I was going through.

"This is so weird," I said to my roommate, my mother, my sisters and brother.

"We know," they responded.

Waking from a coma is not like on television. I would not be ballroom dancing in twenty-four hours.

Mr. Buzz

In my hospital room, beside my bed, was a cord with a small cylinder on the end with a red button on its tip that I could press, which would result in the nurses coming to my room. I would push that button over and over again. It became a routine, and this aggravated the nurses. I do not know why I did it. Perseverance is the name given to such repetitive actions, perhaps. Though pushing the button was meaningless to me, it was not to the nurses.

"Yes Greg," the nurse spoke who was responding to my latest call. She was agitated, by being called for the umpteenth time.

"My diaper is dirty."

She undid my diaper and it was not dirty. This was just something I said a lot to the nurses as an excuse for buzzing them. I could not even tell if I did defecate.

"No it is not," she said.

"Can you give me a boost up please?"

I developed another repetitive habit of squirming down the bed, resulting in my legs not having enough room.

"No! Do it your self," she angrily answered, knowing I could not.

I buzzed again about five minutes later, and this time I did dirty my diaper. The same nurse came.

"My diaper is dirty," I said.

She quickly checked my diaper and then she changed it. Every time a nurse gave me a diaper change, she would wipe me down, use disinfectant, and then towel the area off. This time she did not. She gave me a diaper change but I laid in whatever fecal matter was left after the change.

"Can I have a boost please?"

She did not give me a boost and left. I spent the rest of the night in a crumpled up ball in my own mess. My mind was not capable of remembering which nurse it was, but I did know that I was going to give every nurse a hard time after that. My perseverance now had justification.

Morning came and I was still in an uncomfortable position. Why I was in this position was reminder enough for my actions. I held the condom on my catheter, and by doing so, pressure built up resulting in it bursting and urine spraying in my diaper and on my sheets. I buzzed for a nurse.

"My catheter is broken and my diaper is wet. So help me you -----!"

The words that came from me were those of someone possessed.

It may have been a different nurse as she looked at me with shock in her eyes. She changed my diaper, wiped me down, and gave me clean sheets. She changed my catheter and began to leave. Just as she turned to me to tell me she did not appreciate being talked to like that, I held my catheter again and it burst. After going through the same process again, I asked her for another favour.

"Can you give me a boost please?"

Surprisingly, she did move me up the bed, making me more comfortable.

"Thank you," I said.

'You're welcome."

She left, probably confused at my quick change in temperament. I do not know why I buzzed so often, but I think it was a habit that now had an excuse. I always remembered the mistreatment from that one nurse, and I then used that single instance as an excuse to make it difficult for all the nurses. They would fight back sometimes, but the state I was in must have been expected from my injury. They would sometimes tape my buzzer to the wall so I could not reach it. Once, they had my arms in restraints, but the restraints were removed and never used again after my mother and my very vocal younger sister Melissa stated angrily in horrified distaste, "He is not an animal!" as they discovered me in those arm restraints wearing a diaper, laid out on a gurney in the hallway, with no blankets covering me.

Sometimes, the nurses would wheel me into the hall to keep a better eye on me. I didn't have the power to buzz them from here, but they could not tape my mouth shut. I spoke and hollered so much that they would give me back the buzzer. I guess I won, but I did not know it.

I would develop other habits that stemmed from a single event too. I suppose such habits are expected from a head-injured victim. I did not know that, however, and for the next week, I only remembered those who would help me or abuse me as long as I could link them to something that was essential for my survival or that was to my detriment.

Localized

"Can I please have a drink?" I moaned.

"No, you can't have anything Greg," my mother stated sadly.

My brother and stepfather could not cope with seeing someone they cared for struggle anymore. They were planning some way to give me a drink. The nurse came in to swab my mouth to clear it of germs and mucus. It was a disgusting sight as the nurse put a small sponge attached to a stick into my mouth and cleared it of a syrupy substance. Almost three weeks without brushing my teeth had left my mouth a cave of germs and disease. That moment gave Brian an idea.

He left the room, and when he came back he opened his coat, revealing a can of soda in his inner pocket. I looked up to his face and noticed that he was winking at me and putting his finger to his mouth to give me the signal to be quiet and not to give the nurses any idea of what he was up to. When the nurse left, he took another swab that she had left behind and dipped it into the soda.

"Okay Greg, carefully bite down on the sponge."

I did, and for the first time in twenty days, I got my drink, albeit a small one. I enjoyed it greatly and was thankful for Brian's inventiveness. My brother was also present and started to bring soft drinks too. The following day, Brian and Scott were all I remembered and focused on.

"Where is Scott? Where is Brian?" I questioned.

"They will be here soon," my roommate responded.

They were the key to me getting a drink. Even though they could have gotten into hot water and could have even killed me, they were thrilled with the happiness that the simple task of dipping a sponge in soda pop and giving me a drink was allowing me.

"Scott, line me up another shot," I said.

"Sure thing." My brother chuckled and was proud to be helping me out.

As he placed the sponge in my mouth, I bit down too hard, breaking it off its stick. My mother hopped up to help out as I could choke from the sponge. She and Scott almost lost their fingers, but they were able to get the sponge out of my mouth. The "bar" was closed for the time being, but I persisted in asking for Brian and Scott.

I do not recall ever eating at the general hospital, but apparently my fondness for my stepsister Sharlene grew because of her role in feeding me. My other stepsister, Tonja, was also there, and I had two brothers from my mother's third marriage as well, Tor and Aaron, but I had not met them yet. Tonja allowed me to live with her those first two months that I was out West, and I grew closer to her than Sharlene at that point. However, because Sharlene was the first person that fed me, I asked for her more and forgot about Tonja.

Like the link between drinking and my brother and Brian, Sharlene meant food. I would develop other links and would confuse other people with the person who meant something to my survival. I didn't remember my sisters, for example, but called them Mom or Allison. Mom and Allison were the ones I remembered helping me first, so anybody who helped me received their name.

Another person I remember was Tom. He was a

physiotherapist who, along with an assistant, would stand me up with the aid of a board and make me do stretches with my arms. I was strapped to this cushioned board (tilt table) so I would not fall over, as I did not know how to stand. This procedure was also used to prevent bedsores because I was immobile for twenty-four hours of the day. I do not ever remember being raised to the vertical position using the tilt table, but I do remember finding it frustrating once stood up. Having to stretch out for Tom with my arms weakened me, and being restrained made me feel like Frankenstein's monster. My mannerisms and movements made me look like that monster too.

After Tom and his assistant left, it was time for me to say good-bye to my sisters and brother. I may not have done this right after Tom finished, but it felt like it. I reached out my arms from where I was lying as best I could, and I hugged and said farewells to my sisters, still mistaking them for Mom and my roommate.

"Bye Scoot. You will always be Scoot." I hugged my brother, calling him by his childhood nickname.

"I know, Pudder. I know," he responded, using the nickname he had given me when we were young as well. It was short for pudding head, which was the alias for a pro hockey goal tender. Since I played in goal when we played street hockey growing up, I was called Pudder. I do remember saying good-bye to Scott because I linked him to getting a drink. But I was saddened by the fact that I had forgotten my sisters and was not able to thank them for their love and support. I just hoped I would start remembering people for who they were and not for what they did for me.

41

Starting His work

"Okay, Greg. Sit up," Mom said.

I tried and fell over. I could not even rise to sit up. Mom would sit me up and I would just fall over.

"Allison, when that social worker comes in, Greg has to sit up and look at her and nod to what she is saying. If he doesn't, he may be put into Extended Care instead of the Rehab hospital."

Mom was starting to panic. She and Allison were getting emotional at the thought of me in Extended Care. Whether or not I was routed this way or not was an important factor in the recovery process. If I were placed in Extended Care, therapy would not be a priority and this delay could limit my progress, if indeed there was going to be any progress. I would not be allowed to be a "bed blocker" in the system. As soon as there was any sign as to what your prognosis might be, you were shipped out to free up the space you occupied so that someone else could be quickly judged as to what their chances for future recovery might be. The health care system that Canada is so proud of works like a production line, tossing aside those patients deemed rejects without giving them enough time to continue moving on the healing conveyer belt. With so little time allowed for improvement, I would imagine that there are many in this country that are cast aside as incurable.

My mom and sister tried sitting me up and coached me all week. The social worker had come the previous weekend to see if I was ready for the move to Extended Care or rehab. I fell over and could not even give the impression of comprehending what was being said to me.

"He is the same as last weekend Allison. What are we going to do?"

Allison shrugged her shoulders and said mournfully, "I

don't know."

The general hospital's social worker came in carrying a clipboard and pulled up a chair to the side of my bed. Mother was about to say something when all of a sudden I rose and sat up facing the social worker. I do not know what she was saying, but I looked at her with my empty eyes and nodded whenever there was a break in conversation.

"Well Greg, talk to you later. Thank you," she said.

"You're welcome."

Once the door shut, I fell over. Mom pulled my legs around so I could sleep comfortably. She and Allison looked at each other with amazement. I fell asleep not realizing or remembering what just happened or how important what I did was, at least not consciously. The next day, I needed help rising and sitting up for breakfast, but the day before was the only time it was essential for me to do so. Somehow, I sat up on my own even though I did not know what was going on or even remember the event. God simply knew that I had to leave for rehab if I was to improve, and He made sure I had the opportunity.

Expected rudeness

"Good news, Greg!" my mother said. As usual I did not respond. "In the next couple of days you may be transferred to another hospital for rehabilitation."

"Good."

I gave one-word answers. I did not feel like talking when I was not interested in the topic. I would stare at the wall in my room and still wonder what happened, how I got here in the first place.

I was transferred to another room. It was different from my first room because this one had another occupant. I had a private room previously because I was not tolerant of any noise, and so for the next two days I had to put up with noise for the first time since being injured, adjusting as well as I could to new input.

"I'm going to tell her to shut-up!" I said to Allison as the mother beside us was talking to her son. He too was beaten and in a coma. All that separated us was a curtain.

"Shhh, Greg. She is going through what your mother and I went through," Allison quickly whispered.

"Does this teddy bear look like your aunt? Say hi to your aunty." The mother spoke childishly to her son as he lay there in a coma.

"Humph. Shut up!" I yelled into my pillow.

The one emotion that I retained and showed from the first moments after waking up was extreme anger. Once again Allison told me to try to be considerate.

I had my moments of impoliteness and inappropriateness towards every one.

Allison and my mother, and all those who were involved in my care knew this phase was part of my recovery from head injury and were not bothered by my sudden crude comments and actions. I hoped to recover from not having control over myself.

I tried to stop from saying anything towards my new roommate and I think I succeeded, but I knew that this night was going to be long and hard. Long hard nights were something to which I would have to grow accustomed.

Chapter 4

The other side of life

"Mom, when is the ambulance coming?" I asked.

"In about ten minutes," she responded.

"Mom, when is the ambulance coming?" I asked once again.

She looked at Allison and shrugged her shoulders before repeating what she had just said.

"Mom, can you go see if the ambulance is coming?" I did not ignore what she had said previously out of rudeness but because my mind was only concentrating on one thing and was not capable of understanding more than the ambulance arriving.

"All right. I will go see if it is coming." My mother was willing to put up with what I was going through.

"Allison, can you check to see if Mom is okay?" I asked as the door closed, my mother having just left the room.

"Okay."

The fear of something happening to my mother was unsettling. It was a fear that I had for Allison and my family and friends. Allison and my mother knew about my fear, and they tried to help me through it by doing these things I requested out of fear for them.

"Where is the ambulance?" my mother questioned with a loud enough voice for me to hear.

"I don't see it coming," Allison responded with the same loud voice.

They looked at each other and smiled and continued with the same banter. They knew the relief it brought me. Then the door to my room swung open because the ambulance had arrived. I was transferred from my bed to a gurney, and the two paramedics began to roll me down the hall. I looked up to the ceiling, because I had no other choice, and watched the rows of fluorescent bulbs go by. I was starting to realize that something horrible had happened to me.

The entrance doors to the hospital slid open as I felt the cold fresh air hit me. It felt good because it was something I did not have for almost a month of my life. The paramedics then hoisted me into the ambulance, and before they shut the doors, my mother said that she and Allison would follow and meet me at my destination.

The ride did not take long, and the paramedics opened the doors and hoisted me down. Another set of sliding doors opened. They began to wheel me in and I felt the cool air once again. The doors shut behind me, and it seemed to me that my freedom was lost.

I was awake this time I entered a hospital, not suffering from a coma and amnesia. I was much more aware of my surroundings, and the question of why I was here was now on my mind. I looked down to my left and saw a physically and mentally disabled older woman. She was in a wheelchair and was pointing to the tray attached to it. I looked to where she was pointing and saw a happy face with the word "HI" beneath it. I did not say hi back.

I was then wheeled to my private room and transferred onto my bed. I was more comfortable in the isolation of my own room. I was happy to be on my own, but I fell asleep quickly because the move had exhausted me. However, I would have trouble sleeping in the days to come as I struggled to comprehend why I was in such a place.

Adjusting

I woke up the next day, after my first night of many to be spent at the rehabilitation hospital. But in truth, I only felt like I had awakened frequently, and a lot of what I thought were my dreams, and the conversations that took place in them, were actually real. My mind still could not distinguish between the two states of consciousness.

The Gorge Road Hospital was a four-floored building and catered to neuro-rehab patients and others who had to learn how to fend for themselves once they survived their physical ordeal sufficiently. The hospital also had seventy percent of its space allotted to extended care for those who are not capable of surviving on their own. I was here for rehabilitation, however, to see if I could live on my own or if I would have to live where someone could take care of me.

I was given a wheelchair with an attachable tray that my mother, stepfather Brian, and Allison would set me in and push me through the hallways. Hopefully, through therapy, I would not be dependent on the wheelchair. I remember the first days in the rehabilitation hospital only vaguely. I did not have any therapy as I rested and adjusted to my new home. My mother and Allison wheeled me on my first tour of the hospital.

The population of the rehab floor contained mostly seventy- to eighty-year-old people who had survived a stroke and who, like me, had to learn everything all over again. As I was pushed, I could see their rundown and tired faces. Many would say hi and produce a smile, however. I would not respond because, in the state I was in, I was not capable of smiling or understanding the emotion behind a smile. My voice had no inflection, and even if I could smile and say hi, it would be too tiring. While being pushed, I noticed a kitchen that was used to store patients' drinks or food brought from home.

"Mom," I said.

"Yes."

"May I have something to drink?"

"Sure. What would you like?"

I paused and looked forward. I could not think of what I wanted to drink. I also was startled because I was used to being told no. I looked up to Mom, and she knew I was confused because my mannerisms showed nothing.

"Okay. How about some cranberry juice?" she said.

"Yes please," I responded in my monotone voice.

Before I put the cup to my mouth, I was given instructions on how to drink because I had forgotten how to swallow. The speech and language pathologist had given directions to my mother earlier so that I could have a drink.

"Okay Greg, hold it in your mouth," Mother instructed.

I did.

"Now swallow."

I went through this process, being coached at each step, until my cup was empty. I was unable to take a sequence of gulps and was told after each gulp what I was to do. When I would try to drink quickly, I would choke and then cough, as it would go down the "wrong tube." After my drink, we took one more lap of the floor.

The lap consisted of a square with three-quarters of it silent and empty in the evenings and on the weekends because the social workers, therapists, and doctors had that time off. The other quarter was busy and contained some of the rehab facilities, patients, a lounge with a television, and the nurses' station. My room was across the hall from the lounge. I had a private room. Because of my injury, the smallest of noises would disturb my sleep. I was given an oscillating fan too, which was placed on my nightstand to drown out any noise.

"White noise" is what one of the nurses called the sound created from the fan.

As I was being wheeled into my room after the last lap of the floor, a voice behind me said hi. My mother wheeled me around to face the person it had come from. Surprisingly, I said hi back.

"Hi. My name is Greg."

"My name is Bob."

"Do not forget to entertain strangers, for by so doing some people have entertained angels without knowing it. Remember those in prison as if you were fellow prisoners and those who are mistreated as if yourselves were suffering."
Hebrews 13- 2, 3 (King James Version)

New friends

Bob is a seventy-eight-year-old man who is in a wheelchair because of his inability to walk. When he had triple bypass surgery, an air bubble got into his blood stream and traveled to his spine. When the doctors removed the air bubble, usually a successful procedure, they damaged his spine, leaving him paralyzed. I later would ask Bob why he did not sue or file a claim against the surgeon, and he stated that doctors make mistakes like everyone else. The only difference for doctors is that the smallest of their mistakes receives greater notice than the largest mistakes by most of the rest of us. The doctor who botched his surgery was the same one who tended to me at the general hospital.

"So Greg, what happened to you?" Bob asked.

I did not respond, because I did not know what happened to me, so my mother intervened.

"Greg was walking home from work when he was attacked from behind. The damage resulted in fifteen days in a coma."

It was the first time I heard what happened to me. Actually, it might have been the tenth time, but it went in one ear and out the other. It did not stick from memory loss, because my memory is one thing that was not affected by the trauma to my brain, other than the three and a half weeks of post-traumatic amnesia. And fifteen days of that memory loss were those spent in a coma. Maybe this explanation did not stick because I did not want it to.

"That's horrible. What's wrong with society today?" Bob said, angrily shaking his head and turning to speak to me.

"When you get through this," — Bob did not say if — "me and you are going to form a vigilante group and get these people. Don't you worry." He patted me on the knee.

What an intimidating group that would be!

Bob was the first person I met, at least the first who I remembered, at rehab. I do not know why I turned and talked to Bob, but he was going to help me. In fact, the people I chose to open up to and grew fond of at this hospital did help me. The reasons that my choices paid off in my recovery could only be explained by God knowing which ones could help and which ones could not and working through those who could. I met many people besides Bob, and with meeting them came the horrible stories that brought them here.

Sharon was a young attractive girl who had a stroke because she smoked while on birth control, a combination that did not mix well with her heart problem. Another young lady, Carnie, had a leg amputated because of diabetes. She was so distraught with life that she smoked and ate sweets, not giving a hoot if she died. The people at this hospital all had sad stories to tell, sad stories like mine. Maybe I should be thankful that my mind was in a fog from what had happened to me in my story and thus could not take in all the depression and negativity in these others.

"Just hang in there and smile," Bob said this first time I met him.

"Good night," I said back with a smile that looked and felt like there was a person on each side of me pulling the corners of my mouth up to form one.

After my transfer into bed, which consisted of me wrapping my arms around someone's shoulders and being lifted, I could not sleep. I was trying to put together what I had just seen and heard. Everything I absorbed was unbelievable. I went from walking home from work to waking up in a hospital, and everything, including me, had changed in between. This had to be a bad dream.

As I lay there, I noticed an electrical socket on the wall beside me. I thought that maybe if I shoved my fingernail into it I would wake up from this nightmare. I figured that, just like the cafe blowing up in my previous dream, this death would result in me waking up, in waking to who I was before. I turned my head away from the socket and noticed my mother lying beside me on a pull out cot. She and Allison would take turns sleeping with me and put their lives on hold so I would not be alone. After seeing her there, I was not going to risk losing either of them for a plan that might not work. These women loved me and I loved them. I did not want to risk the chance of not being with them, even if it meant that I could not walk or be the same as I had been before finding myself in the hospital.

Helping hands

I looked at the clock in my room, which reminded me of the clocks in public school. It was very big with long red hands and the minutes marked up to sixty beneath the hours. I would get used to looking at that clock watching time go by. I had no choice. I was on my back most of the time because I could not lie on my stomach. The clock read ten to eight when my mother folded up her cot, moved it into the hallway, and returned with my wheelchair. I was fully always awake whenever I heard my door open, which was followed by the bright light from the hall shining in on the floor.

My diaper was checked and I was given a new one by Mom or Allison whether it was dirty or not. I was then wiped down before the long process of changing from my sleeping attire and into clothes. Putting my shoes on was the most tiring event because of the sitting balance and therefore abdominal strength required to do so. Mom or Allison watched me like a "hawk" and always were there to prevent me from toppling over, as my tendency was to fall to one side. After that, I was then transferred to my wheelchair for breakfast. Before my tray was attached for my breakfast, my mother pushed me to the small sink in the corner of my room to wash myself and brush my teeth.

Brushing my teeth took me a long time before my incident because I am meticulous about oral hygiene, but now it took me maybe a minute because it tired me so much. I could hardly remove the toothpaste cap and squeeze paste out. I would grab a Dixie cup and spit and rinse. Mom or Allison then filled the sink up with warm water and then I would wash my upper body with a cloth. I struggled and had difficulty as I could barely move my stiff arms.

I looked up and saw myself in the mirror above the sink. I looked at my reflection and was perplexed. My eyelids were sagging and I was very thin. My skin looked dirty and old, and my face looked emotionless. The reflection confused me because the confused thoughts in my head were not reflected in the mirror. I felt different all the time, my emotions perhaps not fluctuating normally but still fluctuating, but I could not show emotions on my face.

A nurse brought in my medication with breakfast. My breakfast was set on the tray in front of me, and my mother watched and helped when I needed it. I first took my medication, about twelve different pills, and then began my breakfast. Breakfast was not much: a glass of orange juice, milk, coffee, a piece of soggy toast, and Red River cereal (cream of wheat). Mother fed me a lot of it, but I would attempt new things on my own in the days to come. With breakfast finished, Mom wiped my whole face with a warm cloth.

"Thank you."

"You're Welcome."

Thank you is all I could say to a mother who put her marriage and new life on hold for me. I was very fortunate to have the support system I had in Mom and Allison. Allison quit her job to give my mother a break every other night helping me and sleeping beside me. I did not have the ability to think and comprehend the question of where my father was, but that question was starting to grow deep inside of me, and one day I would need an answer.

"Thank you Mom," I said once again after she pushed me through the door. "Thank you."

Chapter 5

Therapy

After my breakfast, I was pushed to a gymnasium-like room for physiotherapy. Physiotherapy dealt with getting me mobile again, hopefully by ambulation, a fancy word that medical professionals use for walking.

"Hello Greg. My name is Tracey."

Tracey, the physiotherapist, was a younger lady who lifted me and set me on a cushioned table. I was placed on my back as she began to massage and stretch my legs and arms through range of motion exercises. She also made me try to move and help out with the exercises.

Just from the minimal movement I could accomplish at this point, I realized that there was a huge difference between my left and right sides. The first and most severe blow I received from my attack was to the right back of my head. I would find out through Tracey that this part of the brain controls the left side of the body, which explained the difficulty I was having with that part of me. A head injury has the same disabling effects as a stroke, and these effects are most evident in the side of the body opposite the trauma. Being right-hand dominant was not a plus in that it made me neglect my left even more. I attended to my left, but only with cueing. This left-sided neglect would subside if my memory would allow me to remember my left, but at this point in my recovery I had to rely on someone to remind me.

I was sat up, but I could not sit up for long as my lack of balance and strength would cause me to fall over. Tracey kept sitting me up and would put an arm on both sides of me as I tried to balance myself. Through this practice, hopefully I would be able to control and balance myself and become stronger just by the simple act of sitting up. I would always tilt towards the left, the most affected side, and by Tracey just tapping my right shoulder I would use my momentum in that direction to correct myself. I wanted to improve on this to be of more assistance with donning my shoes in the morning.

Tracey worked on my feet while I was sitting up or lying to one side. Her massages and working out the "kinks" might have felt better if numbness was not shooting through parts of my body. The numbness was now in my feet and calves. This numbness had left my hands and moved down my body, which I could not explain and never mentioned. I remembered having great difficulty at the General Hospital with my hands, and I would ask Brian and my brother to crack my fingers to get rid of the numbness.

At ten o'clock, my session with Tracey was over. I was placed in my wheelchair and taken back to my room. I had occupational therapy at eleven thirty, so I would rest until then. Before my mother, Allison, and I returned to my room, however, I wanted a drink. We proceeded to the kitchen by the nurses' station down the hall from my room.

"What would you like to drink?" Mother asked.

"Cranberry juice, please."

I may have had other choices, but cranberry juice stuck in my memory because it was what I had first. While my mother was getting my drink, I looked to the right and noticed a small chalkboard on the wall. It read December 2, and above the date was written the fact that there were twenty-three days until Christmas.

"Allison, what day did this happen to me?"

"November tenth."

I tried to figure out on my own how many days ago it happened. "I have been here for twenty four days?" I questioned.

"You have been here for two days and at the General

Hospital for twenty one," Allison answered.

Mom gave me the drink, and after going through the steps involved in drinking, I gave her my cup back. I looked at my hands set on my wheelchair tray and looked at the chalkboard once again. I had difficulty comprehending the time that had gone by and why I did not have enough strength and ability to wipe the chalkboard clean and have those days back. I just did not know where twenty-three days of my life went.

"Greg, we better take you back to your room for a quick one-hour nap," Mom replied.

I was pushed to my room and transferred to my bed. Twenty-three days of my life were gone and unaccounted for. I did not feel like sleeping

Another Occupation

As I was pushed to occupational therapy, I passed Bob.

"How is it going, buddy?"

I answered back with a shrug of the shoulders, more like a twitch.

"He is doing fine. Thank you for asking," my mother responded.

"Hang in there, Greg," Bob said after I continued on to therapy.

"See you." I muttered.

Occupational therapy focused on the healing of the mind. Such therapy would assess where my writing, speaking, and cognitive abilities, such as memory and attention, as well as perception, stood after my head injury. Through this therapy, whatever functions I had lost would hopefully come back for these functions were important in carrying out the simplest activities of daily life.

"Hi Greg. My name is Paula." Paula was an older lady who seemed very in touch with nature. "Greg, could you tell me the date?" Paula asked.

"December second."

"That is correct. Very good."

Unlike my physiotherapy session, I received a compliment when I got it right even though the compliment was for very little in the way of accomplishment. Tracey, my physiotherapist, concentrated more on the body parts than who they were attached to, making the session quiet and sombre. Not that I was one for talking in the state I was in anyway.

"Thank you."

Right from the start I took a liking to Paula. She seemed to have a better understanding of my situation than most of those around me. She knew that even remembering the date was a big step in my recovery. After introducing herself to Mom and Allison, Paula removed my tray and I was pushed to the head of a table. Mom and Allison sat on both sides of me and Paula gave me a pencil and a paper. The letter S was on the paper in big bold print. Beneath the S there was a series of letters, numbers, and symbols in the same big bold print.

"Okay Greg, what I would like you to do is circle the letter S in each row," Paula instructed.

"Okay."

Easy enough, I thought to myself, and I felt somewhat offended by the test, thinking a person who is college educated should never be submitted to such a test. I had difficulty holding the pencil and circling all the S's, but I finished quickly and handed it to Paula. Paula proceeded to mark the test as I watched. I was curious to see the results and was surprised when I had several wrong. I missed a couple of S's and circled a dollar sign and an ampersand. Paula did not seem surprised and said I would get better with more testing.

I felt upset and realized that there was something wrong with my mind. I still had the same monotonous look on my face, but inside I wept. Three years of going to college and doing quite well might be worth nothing and forgotten because someone attacked me and left me for dead. Even though I felt something like this before my attack too, because all my schooling had resulted in was a job mopping floors.

"Okay Greg. What I am going to give you is a journal so you can write down how your day went, and your mother and Allison can also do writing activities with you. Here is another one for you to try. It is the same S one you did today. This and writing in your journal is your homework for tonight. So I will see you tomorrow at the same time and place."

After she gave me a red folder with blank paper and a pencil, I thanked Paula and said goodbye. My mother and Allison did the same and pushed me back to my room for lunch and an afternoon nap.

"That went well," Mother said.

Allison responded right after with a "Yeah."

I had no response and thought to myself about what went wrong with that "S" activity. Lunch came and Allison and Mom helped me eat as usual. Afterwards I was helped to my bed and stared at the clock. I did not sleep and again talked about how weird my situation was several times.

Looking at the clock made me think of the days back in public school, watching the time go by and waiting for recess. I fared well in public school, but now I could not pass a grade one student's test. I could not even enjoy recess because I did not have the ability to play, or even to learn how to play.

Toilet Training

I woke up from my attempted nap for dinner and medication. My dinner consisted of a piece of bread, a can of ginger ale, pudding, and shepherd's pie in the shape of a scoop of ice cream. Gravy was poured over the scoop and carrots were thrown around it. Along with my dylantin medication, which I was given to prevent seizures, I was also given antibiotics for my urinary infection. I took other pills but did not know what they were for. I also was starting to take strong laxatives because I had not defecated for three days.

I had been in hospitals for almost a month and did not recall defecating. Apparently, I did but lacked the sensation of one coming on. However, I could feel the sensation of urinating. A healthy person would have the ability to feel the urge and hold it until getting to the bathroom. I could not. Whenever I felt the urge to urinate, I just urinated. There was no space between the urge and the action.

"I wet myself," I said in a demeaned tone.

Once I was transferred to my bed, Allison tended to my diaper change. The visions I had before of Allison taking off my pants were not at all like this, and should not be like this, I thought. She took off my hospital pants and removed my diaper. I was then wiped down with disinfectant, which was sprayed on my privates. My concerns about my penis size were not on my mind; all I was worried about now was a clean diaper and not peeing again.

I would be in diapers until I developed the ability to hold it between the urge to urinate and urinating. Even if I could hold it long enough, however, I could not stand. The human body does not just urinate, however, and I guessed that just knowing when I was going to defecate would be a good start. When this occurred, a bedpan would be placed underneath me.

I felt like a baby, helpless and dependent, whenever I was changed and needed assistance for pericare.

Because of this I became obsessed with my bodily functions having greater focus towards continence than even walking. I did not have the insight to realize I would have to stand and walk to be able to get out of diapers. I had to follow the steps of a toddler.

"Okay Greg, Allison will be here tonight. Here is a piss jug, for lack of a better term."

Mother placed a urinal, a blue jug with large opening, on the nightstand by the bed beside the fan. Mom knew I could not use it alone, but just doing that gave me encouragement.

"Good night, honey. I love you."

"I love you. Good night."

Mother left and I worried about her. The hospital was only a block from the apartment I shared with Allison, but the paranoia that something might happen to her was deep in my thoughts. I did not recognize the irony of being attacked, living, and rehabilitating on the same street — or indeed that all of this took place within two blocks on the same street.

It was six o'clock when I was placed into bed after dinner. I was lying down to allow my food to digest and to rest from the act of eating, and I would do so after every meal. At seven o'clock, Allison was going to transfer me to my wheelchair, attach my tray, and take me for a tour of the floor. I was also going to do my homework assignments.

"Okay Greg, get some rest. I will be right here."

In the state I was in, I did not realize how special this was. Not too many friends would sit in the dark and do nothing but watch over you. She could not even read or have a snack as the smallest of noises caused me to snap at whoever was making it. Allison was watching time go by just like me, but she had no reason except that she was here so that I would not have to do it alone. Who knew that this could come from someone with whom you had argued, someone you were going to move away from a couple of months earlier.

"Allison, I wet myself."

Maybe I was thinking of her, giving her something to do.

Adaptation

After my last tour of the evening, I was pushed into my room. Allison always gave me a soft peck on my head while pushing me. Before I crawled into bed, with Allison's assistance, my journal was placed in front of me along with a pencil. I would write the date and then, to the best of my abilities, write what I thought. After I did so, Allison would look at what I wrote and read it aloud.

As I wrote, I realized that my writing skills were never great, legibility wise, but I could not imagine I was ever this bad, as well as language and grammar. Mostly, I could not remember how to write. Allison would watch over my shoulder and tell me if I was not staying between the lines. She would interrupt me several times as I could not seem to concentrate on both what I was writing and staying between the lines.

"Okay Greg, stop writing. You're going beyond the margin."

Not only did I go beyond the margin, I wrote off the page onto the folder and then onto my wheelchair tray. Allison then took a ruler out, took my pencil, and darkened the margins.

"Thank you."

What was running through Allison's mind as she witnessed a friend she had attended college with, and who had a nearly a perfect grade point average, struggle just to write what he thought of today's events and to stay between the lines?

"Greg," she said, as I was about to do it again.

"Thank you," I responded.

I completed my last sentence and tried handing it to Allison. Before the journal fell to the ground, Allison grabbed it and started to read it.

"What I learned on the second was how hard work pay off thru meeting Tracey in physio and Paula in occupational that effort pay off."

"Very good Greg," Allison said after a small pause.

"Thank you."

Allison then put the "circle the S" assignment in front of me. Upon her explaining what to do, I began to circle the S's and started to get it right this time.

"Greg, you are closing your left eye." Allison said.

"I know. I can't control it. It flutters and I can't see."

I finished the assignment and Allison corrected it. I did not have anything wrong this time. Because I was hit on the upper right side of my head, the side that controls the functions for the left side of the body, I could not even control my left eye properly, losing the ability to focus and read. By closing my left eye, my right eye could then focus and interpret what I was looking at.

"Well done Greg. It is getting late. It is almost eight-thirty, so we'd better get some sleep."

Allison took off my tray and transferred me to my bed. My socks were taken off, and because I had wet myself earlier, I was already in my sleeping attire. I was then tucked in, and two thick towel-like mats were placed beneath my behind, so that when I urinated, anything that seeped through my diaper would not cause a change of sheets.

"Good night Greg," Allison stated as she turned on the oscillating fan beside my head.

"Good night."

Once Allison was settled in the cot beside me she was struck by my pillow, followed by a question.

"Can you fluff my pillow please?"

I was able to reach behind my head with my right arm and grab the pillow. She got up and obliged. I had developed the habit of doing this right from when I woke from my coma. I would also call for Allison when I got tangled in my blankets as I rolled onto my side. Such repetitive habits had decreased since my incident, but for now, Allison or Mom would have to get up between a dozen and twenty times per night.

I do not really know how I slept. I would stare at the clock, and it seemed that I watched all night. Maybe I would fall asleep at 9.45 and wake up at 2.45 to begin watching the clock again and not realize five hours had passed. I did have trouble falling asleep initially, and I was given sleeping pills an hour after my bedtime if I was not asleep. Allison would tell me to think of good things and jokingly say to have dreams about sex, which was a good idea with her lying beside me on a cot. If only I had my imagination back.

I had trouble sleeping, but I did not want the night to end, knowing what tomorrow brought. Even though the night dragged on, however, it seemed to be only a blink of an eye before Allison or Mom folded up the cot and the door would open letting in the light and my empty wheelchair, which was not a good reminder that a new day was beginning.

Hard diet

A week had gone by in my new surroundings, and this was my second weekend here. The weekends were used to rest because my therapists had that time off. My sleep would follow the pattern created over the week by my appointments and meals. I would awake at ten minutes to eight for breakfast, which would be followed by a tour or two of the floor. I would always stop for a drink at the kitchen. I now had more than cranberry juice to choose from because Mom stocked the refrigerator with other drinks.

"Greg, how about some eggnog?" Mom asked while Allison pushed me.

"Yes please."

I had not tasted eggnog in years because of its high fat content. I drank quite a bit of it as a teenager and, along with my fast food diet; it had contributed to my ballooning to two hundred and twenty pounds. I tipped the scales at two hundred and thirty after my fun at university, which is extremely heavy for a person who is five foot seven, eight being generous. Through watching what I ate, biking, swimming, jogging, and going to the gym, my weight was more suitable for my height before my attack. I was one hundred and seventy pounds, in the best shape of my life, and not afraid to take off my shirt at the beach.

"After your afternoon sleep, we are going to give you a bath," Mom said after I handed her my Styrofoam cup.

I did not disagree, as I did not remember being bathed in the past month. When we returned to my room for a two-hour sleep before lunch, I surprised Mom and Allison by being able to rise from my wheelchair on my own. I had to put my arms around the neck of whoever helped me because of my poor balance, but I managed the rest on my own.

"That's awesome," Allison stated while Mother responded with, "Great."

"Thank you."

All the stretching and getting the kinks out in physio had helped me. Rising from my chair was not much perhaps, but it was a start. When my lunch arrived and the cover was lifted from my tray, my mother spoke strongly.

"From now on I will go home and make you dinner and bring soups you like for lunch instead of this crap."

She was perturbed by the look of my lunch, and even though I did not care what I ate at the moment, Mom knew I was picky before this happened to me. After lunch, Mom wiped my face and I was put back into my wheelchair. Allison grabbed a fresh diaper and new clothing, and we were on our way to have a bath.

The bathing room consisted of a large tub with controls on a head panel. There was also a funny looking chair. I took off my sweater and Mother and Allison took the rest of my clothes off of me.

"Okay Greg, put your hand around my neck and lift up like you did earlier," Allison said.

I did so and put my hands on a silver safety bar attached to the wall. I was standing, but Allison held me as Mom took off my underwear. There I was, naked to the world, and this time it bothered me some. Nurses would walk in and out to get towels, which were located on a rack in the same room. I did not say anything, however, and my face remained impassive. I was then transferred to that funny looking chair. Allison then fastened a seat belt around my waist. Through repeatedly pushing down on the bar attached to the back of the chair, I started to rise. There was also an electronic scale showing the weight of the person in the chair.

"Greg, you weigh one hundred and thirty pounds," Mother said.

I did not respond. It took me five years to lose fifty pounds, and I had now lost forty in less than a month.

"Allison, can you believe he only weighs a hundred and eighteen pounds," Mom whispered into her ear. Allison just shook her head.

As I was being lowered, there was also a mirror at the head of the tub. I was amazed at how big my arms were but did not realize the fact the rest of me had shrunk. I then looked at my straight narrow face and my hair, which had a shaved spot and small scar where the cranial pressure monitor was inserted. I did not want to look but had to because, if I closed my eyes, my balance was so bad that I would turn over on my side and drown. Allison tampered with the controls and the tub turned into a Jacuzzi.

"Doesn't it feel good?" Mother asked excitedly.

I did not acknowledge what she had said and stared at myself in the mirror. The only thing I thought I had prior to this ordeal, my health, was now gone too.

Chapter 6

Reminding wallpaper

After my bath, I was fastened into the elevating chair and removed from the tub. I then stood with the aid of Mom and the safety bar. While Allison towelled me off, I noticed a full-length mirror to the right of me. I could see my whole body's reflection this time, not just my face and upper body. I could not get a good look because, if I turned my head too far to the right, I would lose my balance and fall over. What little I saw amazed me at how thin, sickly thin, I really was. Before my ordeal, I could just see three ribs on my torso and was quite thick and sturdy.

Now I had to hold onto a bar just to stand, and I could not stand for long because of fatigue, and there were now two more ribs showing beneath the three that showed before. Once Allison clothed me, I was turned to face the mirror while my wheelchair was placed behind me. For the tiniest of moments, I saw the reflection of a person similar to that of a refugee in a war-torn country. This image in the mirror was I, even though I did not believe it could be.

After putting my T-shirt on, Allison pushed me back to my room. When I got there, Mom, who had left as I got out of the tub, decorated my room by taping "get well" cards to the walls. The caring messages were from family and friends, some of them friends I did not know I had and others from whom I had not heard in years. I asked Mom whom the cards were from after I was in my bed.

"This one is from Brian," Mom answered as she pointed a card out.

Brian is my best friend from back East in my hometown of Sault Ste. Marie, Ontario.

"Can you read it please?"

She obliged. Once she got through reading Hallmark's words, she read his:

"Hey buddy. I heard what happened to you and was devastated. I was just visiting you two weeks earlier. I don't know how this could happen. You mean a lot to me and I view you as my brother. I hope, pray, and know you will come through this and look forward to hearing from you. Love, your best friend forever, Brian."

Brian Mandolesi, "Mando", and I were cut from the same cloth even though our upbringings were totally opposite. I am from a large, by today's standards, broken family that was on the verge of becoming lower middle class. Brian is an only child and grew up with both parents, and I admired his father for how he handled himself. Brian's father is the principal of the high school we attended, someone I saw as a role model for how I wanted to be. Mr. Mandolesi and his wife also sent me a card with their deepest sympathies and prayers.

I could not believe the number of cards I had received, or the reasons that I was receiving them. Mom kept reading them and she would tape and tack more to my wall as time went on.

"Who is that big one from?" I asked.

"That is from your boss and staff at the cleaning company. John, your boss, said the staff is going to take up a collection and whatever they come up with he is going to match."

John was close to my age, maybe five years older. He owned and ran the cleaning company. I was envious of him as I thought I probably had the same education as he did and had nothing to show for it except lying in a hospital wondering if I would ever go to the bathroom alone or walk again.

"Tell him thank you."

I had only worked there for two and a half months and knew only John, Colin, and two others. I asked if I received a card from Rhonda, a girl from my hometown who now resided in Vancouver and with whom I was a friend. I had spent a couple of weekends with her before my assault. We went to Whistler, this beautiful ski resort town, and at the moment I was quite fond of her.

"No you have not," Mom said.

"Weird," I replied.

She was also a girl who had a reason to get closer because of what happened to me, but then such a terrible event is also a reason to get away from someone and maybe that is what she wanted. I guess I lost a friend because I wanted more than a friend. My walls were covered with surprises and emptiness, the latter caused by those with whom I thought I was close but who had not bothered to contact me. A hard way to find out who your friends are.

Serious game

By the middle of the week my occupational therapy sessions doubled. I now had another therapy session at two o'clock. The session was with other patients and we all participated in games and exercises. This extra session would test my stamina as well as my concentration and attention in a group setting.

Physically, I was making remarkable progress. I could rise on my own without putting my arms around someone. To get up, I would push down on my legs and rise. Once standing, however, I would need Mom or Allison's assistance to get turned and set in my wheelchair. I now could place my feet on my footrests and push them down from their folding position. I could control the brakes on my own but still had to have Mom or Allison push me. I never wanted to learn how to manoeuvre the wheelchair though. Someone knew I did not need to.

"Okay Greg, take off your shoes," Tracey said to start my

physiotherapy.

"Pardon?" I responded with an attempted glare at her. In the previous sessions, Tracey would take my shoes off

"Well?"

To my mother's surprise, as well as mine, I did. It took me about five minutes, and I almost fell over bending to reach them, but I managed. I felt awkward because my legs were extremely heavy and like dead weight as I folded one over the other to undo the laces. I had my frustration tested undoing my left because my foot did not want to be off the ground.

"Very good Greg," Tracey said while beginning to massage my feet.

By the end of the session, I was exhausted. This time Tracey helped me with my shoes. She then watched me rise on my own. She noticed how I pushed down on my legs to do so and mentioned how we would try to fix it so that I could get up on my own without the aid of momentum from pushing down.

"You are doing very well, Greg. So try not to be so serious and have some fun."

I looked at Tracey with a face that wanted to show anger and speak with anger. "I do not find this fun. Trying to walk again is serious business to me."

Mother turned me around and looked back at Tracey, shrugging her shoulders and mouthing the words of apology.

"Bye Tracey," I said lifting my right hand.

"Bye."

When I returned to my room for my one-hour nap before my first occupational therapy session, I remained awake, not even trying to sleep.

"What's wrong, Greg?" Mom asked.

"Nothing. I'm just thinking."

I did that a lot: thinking about what was next on the list to be tested, thinking about whether or not I would walk again or get out of diapers. I was thinking of things that I knew how to do before and involved no thought. I had taken walking and other simple events for granted: brushing my teeth, untying my shoes, writing my name, showing emotions like laughing and crying, making and eating meals. These were just a few of my thoughts while I stared at the get well cards that covered the wall of my room.

Isolation

"Hello Greg. I'm Jennifer." Jennifer sat at the table with Paula, my occupational therapist. She was dressed more formally and observed the group I was part of while writing notes as we carried on with our exercises.

"We have a new member to our group. This is Greg," Paula said.

"Hello, I'm Stuart."

"Hello, I'm Dot."

"Hello, I'm Julie."

"Hi, I'm Greg."

I did not raise my head to look at them because I did not want them to see me and I did not want to be there. The only people I wanted to talk to and deal with were Allison, Mom and the therapists who were helping me to try to forget this mess. I told my mother earlier in the week that I did not want any visitors and didn't want to talk to anybody. I did not want anybody to see me like this. I was starting to realize that I had a fight ahead of me and was still confused as to why I was having this fight.

"Greg, could you tell us the date."

"December ninth."

"Good. Okay people, with the pencil and paper I have given you, I want you to write as many words you can that begin with the letter 't.' Do this when I say go. You will have fifteen seconds. Okay, go!"

I wrote my words but became irritated by the movement and noise around me as I tried to concentrate. I was gripping my pencil so hard I thought I was going to break it, but with the lack of strength I had I could not break wind. I was getting fed up at being asked the date before every session. I wanted to tell Paula to get her own calendar.

The anger that was prevalent even when I first woke from my coma was brewing inside, and I was even more angered by the fact that I did not have the power to show it. Previously, how I acted and spoke may have given the impression of anger, rage I could not control. Now, I just wanted to rise from my wheelchair, flip over the table I was sitting at, march out of the hospital and go to the Gorge Bridge and pummel the next person who walked over it. That was the type of anger I wanted to show.

At the end of listing words that begin with a certain letter, we were given another sheet with a maze on it. It looked like the back of a kid's menu found at a cheap restaurant. I could not do it. My left eye was so out of control that it blurred my vision. I tried closing it, but when I did I could not turn my head and see the whole maze. I placed my pencil on my sheet and pushed it forward to the center of the table.

"Sorry. I cannot do it."

"That's all right. You did excellent at the word games," Paula said.

"Thank you."

Once the group completed the mazes, we were allowed to go back to our rooms. I wanted to get back. I was tired physically and mentally and wanted to lie down. Once I was in bed, I fell asleep surprisingly quickly. I dreamt I was looking over notes at that same coffee shop along my early morning route. In the dream, I opened my wallet and came across my paycheck, which was quite substantial. I must have had a good job. I then looked at my finger. My finger had a wedding band on it. I looked up and saw this beautiful girl standing before me.

"Hey Greg."

"Hello."

"Hey Greg."

Allison started to shake me to get me up for supper. I responded by punching her in the face.

"I don't want to go to therapy!"

Upon realizing what I had done, my anger was replaced by tragic apology. My glancing blow did not hurt Allison. My attempted punch was awkward and the force behind it could not hurt a fly. To me, however, it felt like I had hit her very hard.

"I'm sorry, Allison. I am so sorry."

"That's okay, Greg. I know you did not mean it."

Mother entered the room and I told her what I had done to Allison and how sorry I was. Allison whispered to Mom what happened and that it was not a big deal, as the two knew of my pendulum-like mood swings. To me, my actions were a signal not to let anger control me.

I was scared because I am not normally the quick-tempered person I was becoming. I could not feel my emotions coming on and did not know how to control them. I struck a girl, something I vowed never to do after my upbringing.

Whatever anger was coming back was returning at full strength, and it was up to me to control it and to know when showing anger was appropriate to the situation and how much anger was acceptable. I made a point to try my hardest to cover up my anger and not to direct it at those who had nothing to do with it. Healthy or not, from that point on it would be me and only me dealing with my anger.

Unnoticed improvement

I woke up from my night's sleep, although I felt as if I had been awake the whole time. My mother helped me change into one of the many pairs of track pants I had and a T-shirt. Before she handed me the shirt, she pushed me to the small sink in my room for my attempt at oral hygiene.

I could brush my teeth on my own and would try to use my left arm for grabbing things. My right was starting to become stronger compared to my left, so I concentrated on my left. Once I finished brushing my teeth, I was given a face cloth and bar of soap. I filled the sink with warm water and wiped my face and upper body with the cloth and soap. I wanted to cry as I haphazardly washed myself. I could not believe I went from showering and brushing my teeth properly to this.

Afterwards, I put on my T-shirt and my mother commented on how well I had done at preparing for a new day. It was the start of my third week in the rehabilitation process, and I was becoming more able to move my body freely and with purpose. I did not notice the accomplishment, however, because I was doing things that involved no thought before my head injury. Now I had to learn these things all over again by recalling the times I could brush my teeth or get washed and dressed for the next day. I was not used to any of this effort for so small a reward.

In physiotherapy, Tracey concentrated on my pelvic joints and abdominal muscles as they controlled my legs. That region was stiff from being immobile, and with my therapy concentrating on that area, I was now able to stand by creating my own momentum without using my arms to push down. I could also turn without falling when I stood.

In my occupational therapy sessions, I was becoming used to the noise and started talking to my group members. I was opening up and did not always look down. I was starting to excel at the word games and other thinking games. My eyesight was still horrible from not being able to control my left eye, however, and I had difficulty with the mazes and exercises with smaller print.

I was now going to begin another session this week. This session dealt with more challenging activities and audio exercises. I did not realize how good I was doing in occupational therapy or that I was advancing to tougher sessions because of my progress. I guess doing, to me, grade three tests and getting them correct was not a big deal. I felt that I had fallen behind, way behind, declining from my high grade point average in college to this. I also seemed to forget that my brain had taken several severe blows and was shut off for fifteen days.

After my physiotherapy, Mother and I returned to my room for my hour and a half of sleep. I lay awake, however, thinking for the first time about how far I had come physically because I could now see and feel my improvement. My naptime seemed to fly by, and Mother started to brush her hair and fix herself in the mirror above the sink, getting ready for my next therapy session.

I now could sit up and stand up, so I thought I would get in my wheelchair and surprise Mom. I sat up and stood up. God, she would be impressed, I thought to myself. This would be a way of showing her that I appreciated all her help and that it was paying off. I was starting to get excited.

I took my first step since my walk home from work, but when I did, I lost my balance and fell flat on my face. Luckily I was able to get my arms in front of me to absorb the fall. The slapping of flesh on the floor caused my mother to turn around and see me lying on the floor. I felt the grainy, pebbly dirt on the floor as my cheek was now on it.

"Oh my goodness, Greg! The nurses will think I am not looking after you." The nurses at the hospital gave me my breakfast and medication, nothing else. Mom or Allison did the rest, which the nurses did not mind because it lightened their workload.

My mother spoke those words frantically while putting her arms around me, straddling my torso with her legs, and trying to lift me off the floor. She succeeded with great difficulty and set me in my wheelchair. My first step reminded me that I still could not walk and eliminated the thoughts about my vast physical improvement. My first step also told me that I should wait until I had relearned the process and was physically able to walk.

My fall did not upset me, however. I was like a large baby taking his first step, albeit a baby with twenty-three years of walking experience. I did fall like a baby but did not cry like one. Maybe knowing I had that experience previously reassured me that I would walk again. Or maybe I just could not cry.

Chapter 7

Added frustration

"Hello Greg. My name is Stephanie."

Stephanie was my therapist for my new occupational therapy session. Two other patients and I sat around a table with Stephanie, and there was a small radio at the head of the table. I was given a folder containing a variety of sheets. Each sheet had different columns with the headings of date, time, errors and test score. One sheet was for audio exercises. After being introduced to the others, we began the therapy. Mom and Allison were allowed to sit in.

"Okay Greg. The woman on the tape is going to say numbers. What you are going to do is tap on the table with this pencil whenever you hear numbers in ascending order." Stephanie noticed a bit of a confused look on my face because a bit was all I could show.

"What do you mean by ascending?" I questioned.

"One, two, three, four and so on, not backwards."

I nodded to indicate that I understood.

"She will go over the instructions once more before the exercise begins. I will mark your misses, incorrect taps, and if your tap was late. I am now going to play the tape, so be prepared."

As she hit the play button on the tape player, I felt nervous, the first time I had that feeling in months. The lady on the tape finished with the instructions and began listing numbers.

"Eight, seven, six, five, six, seven."

I tapped correctly but was late on the next tap, as I did not realize she would list a few in a row.

"Eight, nine, ten, nine, ten, eleven, ten, nine, eleven,"

I missed a few because I would get frustrated at missing one and not concentrate on the exercise. When the exercise was over, I had four mistakes, two misses and two delayed responses. I was angry with myself as I recorded my results on my sheet. Stephanie commented that I did quite well for a first attempt. I also got satisfaction when one of the other participants did poorly. The competitive nature in me was revealed for the first time in a while. Each person got to mark the others when they tried the audio exercise to show if we were paying attention when we were not involved. I certainly was paying attention because I wanted to be the best. I was not the best this day, but I was ultimately very satisfied with doing better than anybody else in the group.

Looking back, I knew that this was wrong of me because I had not recognized the feelings of the others when they did poorly. I had hoped I would remember to do so from now on, but I could not because my injured brain was not capable. Nervousness, frustration, and competitiveness were the three new emotions I had felt because of this exercise, however. Although these are not wonderful emotions to get back first, they seemed to go along with my new temper somehow.

After doing two other exercises, we were finished and I was quite tired. I was exhausted mentally from all the new emotions I had experienced. My mother pushed me to my room, and I stopped our progress at the kitchen for my usual drink request.

"Could I have chocolate milk please?"

When my mother poured my chocolate milk, I noticed my name written on the carton. I asked what the labelling was for.

"Other people store things in here and people take what isn't theirs," Mother responded.

When I was finished, I was pushed to my room. Before we got there, an older man wheeled by.

"Mom, aren't those my pants?" I asked.

"Yes, they are. I guess I should put your name on your clothes too because all patients can use the laundry room and may get your things confused with theirs."

We continued on and another older man passed.

"Mom, isn't that my shirt?"

"Yes. I am afraid so."

When we got to my room, Mother pushed me inside as I felt a new emotion for the first time. Even though I did not show it, I felt it: laughter.

Homemade

"Good news, Greg. Allison and I just had a discussion with the doctors and therapists, and they have given us the okay to bring you home for the day on Wednesday. If the day goes well, you can spend the weekend at home."

Allison and Mom would step out once a week while I napped and attend these multi-disciplinary meetings. All the therapists and healthcare professionals involved with my rehabilitation would discuss how I was recovering and decide what was next. The meeting displayed how my independence was truly lost, because five people were now in charge of what I was capable of doing next.

"Great," I responded to Mom.

I was more anxious than excited to go home, a home that never brought me too much happiness. It made me wonder why I had made the choice to come out here in the first place, because I was not excelling in the months before my attack, to put it mildly, in my goal of making a name for myself.

"Brent, Tonja's boyfriend, gave you guys a used couch and I purchased a table," Mom said enthusiastically.

When I moved out West, I had what I could carry, which was not much: my clothes, compact discs, and Discman. I had my bike sent through the mail. Allison, on the other hand, had many more things and had a moving company bring her belongings out. Her room had a bed, a large desk with personal computer and printer, a makeup table, and a hutch with dresser drawers. Mine had the futon mattress and a milk carton turned on its side for my nightstand. Tonja, who gave me the mattress, also gave me utensils, a pot, and frying pan. Allison and I did not have the means to decorate our apartment and just sat on an inflatable mattress, which my mother had given to me, and watched her television in our bare living room and dining room. The television was quite small, and my brother called it the "postage stamp" when he was visiting.

The apartment and condominium complex were quite nice. It annoyed me that I could not afford to furnish the apartment, but I was going to when I started work at the department store in the menswear section on the Tuesday following the day I was attacked, which of course changed everything. Through working some cleaning shifts, in addition to my new job, I was thinking of buying a used sofa. I was excited to see what Mom did to the place but was also depressed about going back to a place that showed me I had failed. I was also curious to see if I remembered the apartment or the complex at all. My memory had not been affected other than for the first month in the hospital, but I wanted to put it to some use other than the tests I did not understand.

"After your session with Stephanie, we are going to help Sharon make ginger snaps," Mom said. Sharon is the girl I had met earlier and came to know by being a participant in Stephanie's sessions.

"Hello Greg. My name is Deb." Deb is another occupational therapist who focused on life skills such as cooking and grocery shopping, skills needed to live on your own.

"Okay Greg. Sharon is going to make the batter and you are going to roll them into balls and place them on this cookie sheet. If that is all right?"

"Sure."

The batter was more like paste, and as I rolled it into balls, it stuck to my hand and fingers. It was frustrating, and this showed by the size of my last three balls. Those ginger snaps could feed several people. After washing up, Mom pushed me to my room and helped me into bed. Allison then arrived and Mom left for our apartment.

"Greg, I will be back in a couple of hours. I'm going to bring back chicken cacciatore and more drinks. Love you."

Mom gave me her usual peck on the cheek and left. Allison continued giving me small kisses to the back of the head and did so whenever she was pushing me in my wheelchair. I told her that it perturbed me, but then I asked her to continue doing it. I think the love that was shown by these little gestures was helping in my recovery. Even though I lost such emotions because of my head injury, I was starting to become aware of the power of love and its healing abilities.

I was now also becoming aware of the differences in men and women. I noticed that the support given to other patients in the hospital was from a wife, sister, daughter, aunt, grandmother, or girlfriend. My therapist and nurses were also predominantly female. I was realizing this aspect of my surroundings and understood that women are more compassionate, caring, and greatest of all, stronger in the face of adversity. Analyzing and noticing such a thing was a sign that I was becoming healthier mentally.

True to their caring instinct, Allison and Mom would go home about two hours before the hospital's scheduled supper and make dinner for them and for me. Mostly, Mother was going home because the last thing Allison made was so rich it caused me indigestion, another addition to my ailments that I did not need. The dish was tasty though. That is one thing I did remember about the apartment I shared with Allison:

something so delicious and made with such effort was never created in any kitchen where I was the only occupant, unless you consider liver and baked beans exquisite.

Trying motivation

Going home, the mention of pool therapy, baking and cooking meant that I was starting to recover. I did not have to write in a journal any more and was starting to do mental exercises that gave Mom and Allison difficulty.

My eyesight was still horrible but not utterly horrendous, and that was a sign that my brain was healing. Paula, my main occupational therapist, was wonderful about setting up appointments and doing things for me. She was going to have my eyesight tested to see if I needed glasses, but we still had to wait a while because the brain takes time to heal, and it heals at its own pace.

The numbness, which was first in my feet and hands, had now traveled up my legs and was in my lower back and rear. I thought that hopefully, in time, the way the numbness was traveling it would move from my feet, through my body and leave through my head.

I was now aware of my urination and was able to stand while holding on to Mom or Allison to urinate in a bottle (urinal) meant for such a thing. This was the "piss jug," as Mom, Allison, and I would refer to it. I still needed diapers, because in certain urinating situations, I was unable to hold or control myself long enough to stand and use the jug. I would say, "I have to pee," and Allison or Mom would help me up and balance me and hold the piss jug. This was yet another task I demanded of these two, added to wanting my pillow fluffed, blankets adjusted, or a hoist to lift myself up in the bed to make myself more comfortable.

Unlike before I was now aware of my need to defecate.

Such a thing was painful, as I was not sitting on a toilet with gravity to help me. I was lying straight on my back, bedpan beneath me, which made defecation difficult. Mom and Allison never adjusted my bed so I would be in a more sitting position. I would have told them but was not accustomed to the process and was not coherent enough to understand the laws of gravity.

"I'm done, Mom."

"Holy crap, pun intended," Mom said when she went to clean out the bedpan.

When she returned, I said, "Mom, for all those people who want nice abs, just tell them to crap lying down."

Even though I still could not laugh, the feelings were there and my sense of humour, crude as it may have manifested itself, was returning.

I was not walking yet because my joints were still stiff and my mind still had difficulty comprehending the concept of learning how to walk and what commands to give to my legs. I could sit up, stand, and turn around with assistance for balance, and I was improving. I never had those feelings of excitement, nor showed them while improving, however. Mom, Allison, and Brian, who visited on the weekends, would be extremely enthused by my improvements, but that still did not motivate me.

Maybe I had help from someone else to motivate me, inside of me, a silent partner. I just did what I was capable of doing, learning from hard experiences when I would try and push myself, like when I tried to walk on my own. Being applauded and congratulated for such things as standing, going to the washroom, and bathing was not what I was used to. I never received such recognition in twenty-four years of my life. No, make that twenty-two. I suppose that I did get that recognition when I was an infant and toddler but cannot recall it.

Helpful reminders

"Greg, watch it. Be careful," Mother said.

It was snowing, which was strange for Victoria, as it was known for its mild winters compared to other parts of Canada. This added to the strangeness of my situation, making it seem unbelievable. Brian folded up my wheelchair and placed it in the trunk of my mother's four-door compact car. There was even concern, from my doctors and therapists, about how I would react to the drive home.

"Greg, when you get out of the hospital, Brian and I have decided to give you my car so you and Allison do not have to walk around at night."

"Thank you, Mom."

"You're welcome."

The thought of driving again never concerned me. I did not drive in the four months prior to my incident. I never had a vehicle, and now, at the age of twenty-four, I had my first car. I never thought this would be the way I would get it. I guess I should have been excited, but there would be a chance I would never drive again, and in fact, the chance of not walking again was obviously a more important concern for me.

We pulled into the parking lot of the condo complex. My memory did not let me down, as the complex looked familiar. After setting up my wheelchair, I transferred out of the car with Mom and Allison's assistance. Once placed in the chair, I was pushed into our building. A tenant held the door open and the gentleman did look familiar.

"Thank you," Allison said.

The man had the look of shock and sadness, I suppose because he had only seen me jogging, biking, swimming, and getting the mail and was not used to seeing me sickly thin, straight faced, and in a wheelchair. Word had gotten out and spread through the four buildings in the complex that someone who lived amongst them was brutally attacked and nearly beaten to death. I was the crime of the week in the newspaper and on *Crime Stoppers* on television, which included a re-enactment of what may have happened that night. A celebrity now lived with them. I could just imagine the stories about me. And now this gentleman would, I was sure, add to the fables that I did not even know yet but was sure were untrue. I still did not know what happened, so I could not even straighten out these tales.

We entered apartment 406. It did look different from what I remembered because it was. Mother's addition of table with chairs and the used sofa took away the bareness of the apartment that I knew.

"Mom, can I go to the washroom and take a nap before supper?"

"Sure."

I stood over the toilet with Mom's assistance.

"I have to crap too," I said.

"Okay. Well let's try the toilet. I will leave you be, and you can just call me when you are done."

"Thank you."

While sitting, I looked into the closet in my bathroom. The closet had a washer and dryer hook up, but since Allison and I could not afford them so I used it for storage. Everything in it was the same. I did not know how my complete memory was, but I did remember the things in that closet. From my laundry basket, golf clubs, folded old sweaters, to the T-shirts found on the top and only shelf. It gave me the chills, more like an eerie feeling, like things both were and were not as I remembered; or maybe like I was a different person from the man with these memories.

"I'm done, Mom."

"Did you wipe?"

"Yes."

I enjoyed having a normal bathroom experience. The basic actions in life, like taking a dump, now seemed so complicated in my life. When Mom asked if I had wiped myself, I was happy that I did and hopefully would not need the reminder down the road. Like everything I relearned, the activity was broken down into the simplest steps so I could follow them. I had never looked at these activities of daily life this way before and now had a greater appreciation for them. I was also frustrated by the constant instructions, however, seemingly for everything I did. It wore on me, but I realized I needed such information to relearn these things well enough to do them independently. After the bathroom, I moved to my room, which was located just across the hall. With Mom beside me, and the use of the walls to balance, I slowly made it to my bed.

"Okay Greg. We've got to do this slowly. Carefully drop to your knees, and once you're on them, I will help you fall over to lie down."

I just had the old futon mattress lying on the floor, which acted as my bed. Mother had added a sheet of foam and thick blankets to add to its comfort, however, so it was different from before.

"Thank you, Mom."

"You're very welcome. Now have a good sleep. Love you." Mother then kissed me and told me to call her if I needed anything as she shut the door.

My closet doors were open, like the closet in my bathroom, and I remembered everything. Those eerie feelings I had were now changed to hope. Being able to accurately recollect my apartment and its contents suggested to me that maybe what I had experienced, the horrible crime someone had inflicted upon me, did not happen. I fell asleep in a hurry, hoping that when I woke I would be back to how I was before.

"Greg."

"Yes," I answered with as much anxiousness as I could

muster.

"Dinner is ready," Allison said.

I went to get up and I could not. I kept on trying but did not have the strength or the ability to rise from the floor. Allison entered my bedroom, saw me struggling, and spoke. "Hold it Greg. Just grab onto my shoulders and use me to get up."

I did so, and the door opened to reveal my stepfather behind my wheelchair. I sat down and Brian pushed me to the dining room table. That was one thing I did not remember about my apartment; it was wheelchair accessible.

Chapter 8

Homesick

I sat at the new table, a poker table, in our dining room. We all had our dinner in front of us and we began to eat. It was the first time since my ordeal that I had eaten at home and was able to add to the dinner conversation. I was improving socially and spoke more than just a sentence at a time. I could have done so earlier but did not have the strength or desire to speak more than a sentence.

"Why did this happen?" I questioned.

"Well Greg," Mother began, "there are people, sick, evil, people who just don't care about others."

"Greg, God gives us a choice of being good or evil. And the person or people who did this to you chose the latter," Brian added.

Brian is a religious man, if you call a person who attends church and growth groups, and reads the Bible religious. His faith and knowledge had helped Mom during those first tenuous moments at the General Hospital.

"But why?"

I asked why but meant what, when, and even wondered if this had happened. I still had difficulty believing any of my new reality was true.

"Greg, you just have to move on. I know it is hard with what you went through, but life goes on," Allison stated.

"Greg, you have to try and forgive the person or the people who did this," Brian said.

I was confused and angered. How the hell was I supposed to forgive whoever did this to me, those responsible for changing me forever? Both Allison and I looked at Brian as if to say, "Yeah right!"

"It will take time, Greg. I know that I still have faint feelings of wanting to get the people who did this to you and beat them nearly to death like they did to you, but you cannot take such things on," Mom said.

I was confused even more as Brian, Mom, and Allison all referred to the people or person who did this to me. I guessed that they did not even know what happened to me, but how could they?

As Brian began to speak again, Mother interrupted, "Give him time, Brian. We are not in his shoes, and pressuring him to forgive and forget is not the proper thing to do at this moment."

Mom knew of God's work in my ordeal through her previous experiences when I was near death. When Brian told her to give my situation to God, He took it and I awoke. She knew I was not capable of understanding such a thing as deep as that. I did know God was the driving force in my recovery, however. I knew He was working in those around me, from Mom and Allison to the healthcare professionals at the rehabilitation hospital. I would discover later that other events occurred and other people were brought into my life to help me and prepare me for the consequences of this life-altering event. This was His work.

After silence, just the four of us concentrating on eating, I asked Allison a question. "So Allison, is that ghost still in your room?"

Allison was a bit startled that I remembered such a thing. When we first moved in, Allison found out the person, an elderly woman who lived here before us, had died in the bathroom attached to her bedroom.

"Well, every other night that I am home, I have some Bailey's and coffee and fall asleep on the couch."

"I still can't believe you think this place is haunted," I said.

"Screw you. It is!" Allison said, chuckling.

It was nice to be home and not at the hospital. I was feeling happy. I was smiling without effort for the first time as the four of us conversed and finished our supper.

"Well Greg, it is time to head back," Mom said.

"Diane, I will stay with Greg tonight so you and Brian can have some time alone."

"Thank you Allison," Mother replied.

The four of us packed into the car and headed back to the hospital. When we arrived, we got settled back into my room and the four of us decided to go for my usual tour of the rehabilitation part of the hospital where I lived. We came upon the long, straight, quiet hallway where the doctors' and administration offices were located. Between the doors of the offices there were photos of people. There was a maintenance worker at the end of the hall putting up a new photo.

"Remember her, Greg? She was the lady who had stickers on her wheelchair tray that said hi and others things. She would point at them," Allison said as we looked at the photo.

The picture was of the first patient I saw at this hospital. I remembered this because I was starting to be able to remember such things, those things that were memorable. I would not forget those automatic doors sliding open and seeing my disabled door person greeting me in the only way she knew how.

"Did she get discharged?" Mother asked.

"No, she passed away," the maintenance worker replied and continued on with his work.

"Ahhh." Mom and Allison moaned.

I am sure they realized that the numerous photos of people found in this long hallway were dedications. Death is not blind to circumstances. It happens everywhere, including in the apartment I shared with Allison. At this hospital, it is just more prevalent. I started to feel sad, but my face showed the straight emotionless state it had since I arrived at this hospital. I now knew that I could be happy once again, however, that I would feel strongly again. I missed home.

Baby steps

Mom and Brian were in my room when I awoke for my morning routine and breakfast. I had difficulty sleeping because the thoughts of being home were still in my mind.

"Allison, why don't you go home and freshen up," Mom said.

"Good idea. Bye Greg. Love you."

"Bye," I responded.

"Did you have a good night's sleep?" Mom asked.

"Not really." I was eager to get to work and go to my therapy.

"Well Greg, I will see you sometime next week. So keep up the good work," Brian said.

"Bye. Take care," I said.

"You stay in bed and I will be right back," Mom said.

I was already sitting up and dressed and washed for the day. My shoes were set on the bed by my mom before she left to see Brian off. I grabbed them and put them on. I struggled with my balance as I bent over to tighten a shoe. I almost fell headfirst but was able to throw my weight successfully back to prevent it. Now that my shoes were on, I looked at my empty wheelchair at the end of my bed. I remembered what happened before when I tried to get in it by myself, but this did not stop me. I stood up, teetering slightly, but I maintained my balance. I slid my foot forward, lifting it slightly. When I did lift it, I lost my balance and slid my other foot forward.

I moved one and a half feet and stood in front of my wheelchair. I had taken a step but did not realize how special it was because it felt new and awkward. I then turned and fell back into my wheelchair. I let out an "uumph" as my bottom

91

hit the wheelchair, but I was in it. I unfolded my footrests and set my feet on them. I was ready to go.

"Well Greg, Brian is not going to be here this weekend because of work, but he said he will..." Mother stopped speaking because she realized I was not still on the bed.

"Greg, how the heck did you get over there?"

I shrugged my shoulders, not really knowing what I had accomplished. A tear rolled down Mom's face as she hugged me.

"Good for you."

"So when is Brian coming again?" I said.

"In a week and a half, for Christmas. I still can't believe you got up and in your wheelchair on your own."

"Well, we better get going to physio," I said.

"Okay."

Mother pushed me to therapy, still shocked by what had just happened. I never pushed the wheelchair on my own, and for some reason I had not wanted to learn to do so since I arrived at the rehabilitation hospital. When we got to physiotherapy, Mother told Tracey the news.

"Good for you, Greg. Can you take off your shoes and get on this table?"

I did not respond but did what she asked. Tracey was even amazed at my sudden ability to stand up and move even a couple of feet. I do not know what made me take my first steps. All I knew was that I was tired.

Carried away

"Here are your pills, Greg."

Mother handed me a small disposable paper container that held eight pills. I thought she would be really impressed if I took them all at once. I had taken them two at a time before, but I thought, hey things are improving, so why not do this to impress even more? I succeeded and Mother was more shocked and worried about me choking than being impressed. I also scraped the back of my throat, leaving an itch I would have to deal with for a while, another small reminder that I needed to take it slowly.

"While you are resting after your physio, Allison and I are going to have a meeting with the doctors and therapists to see if you can go home for the weekend," Mom said.

This was another of the weekly meetings that Mom and Allison attended regularly that focused on my improvement and what lay ahead. I was anxious to find out if I could indeed go home, because my only visit to the apartment really stirred up feelings of being normal, of at least functioning on my own.

"Okay Greg, what we are going to do is a test to determine how you are recovering and what areas need more focus. You will be marked out of four for each exercise, and you will have this same test later to see how you have improved."

Tracey was clear with her instructions, and I was not nervous because I had developed tremendous confidence over the previous twenty-four hours. I was able to stand on my own and move a few feet if I had something close by to grab onto for the needed support.

"Okay Greg, stand up." I did so, but I used my arms to push down on my legs for momentum.

"Can I do that again?" I asked.

"Sure," Tracey responded. This time I succeeded without pushing down on my legs and was now standing. "Good Greg. Now that you are standing, let's see how long you can stand."

A half a minute went by and just as Tracey started to indicate her approval I fell back and sat on the cushioned table behind me. "That is fine Greg. You are doing well. What I would like you to do is pick one foot up and set it on this stool." Tracey put a half-foot high, four-legged stool in front of me. I picked up my left foot and placed it on the stool.

"Good Greg. Now the right." I did the same thing, but I had to make two attempts at it as I swayed after missing my first attempt and had to regain my balance.

"Now Greg I would like you to stand on one foot and try to remain standing on one foot as long as possible. I will be marking two things: if you can accomplish this task and the length of time on one foot if you do."

I decided to lift my left first. My right leg seemed stronger and did better on the stool test. I lifted my left and held it up for about three seconds before losing my balance. I then tried lifting my right. I was able to lift it but could not hold it off the ground for any length of time. I kept on trying but gave up when the repeated lifting and dropping of my foot started to sound like a tap dancer.

After doing a variety of tests that included such tasks as holding one arm up in the air at a time for as long as I could, I was finished. Out of a possible fifty-six marks, consisting of fourteen tests out of four, I received a forty-six. I thought I had done pretty well, but I did not know getting a mark deducted and scoring three out of four was equivalent to just getting it wrong. I guess it was better to hear forty-six than four.

"Greg, you did well," Tracey stated.

"Thank you."

"You're welcome." I left feeling confident and very proud of myself, content even, but of course without knowing the scoring system.

"Okay Greg, while you have your nap before occupational therapy, Allison and I will be at the meeting I told you about earlier," Mom said on our way back to my room.

After I was settled into bed and they left, I could not sleep. I wanted so badly to go home for the weekend. I watched the clock and knew that by eleven o'clock they would be back with the news. At five to eleven I wet my diaper because I was excited, not because I could not hold it.

"Well Greg, good news. We are going home tomorrow," Allison said.

"Great, I peed myself."

This time peeing myself did not take away from the moment, however. I was going home.

Chapter 9

48 Hours

Saturday morning arrived and I was going home until Monday morning. Mom, Allison, and I had to "run around" before we would finally get home.

"Once we get you into the car Greg, Allison will bring your wheelchair back in and we will go to The Red Cross and get another. We will also get you a shower bench so you can shower," Mom said, as she was always very organized.

"Here are Greg's meds," the nurse said, handing my mother two small envelopes one for each day.

"Bye," I said to the nurse.

She responded with, "Have a fun weekend Greg," and seemed to be touched by my goodbye.

Unlike the nurses at the General Hospital, I was quite fond of the nurses here. It was not that the nurses at the General Hospital did not do their job, other than a few mistreatments worthy of *60 Minutes*, but rather, it was that I was coming out of my fog and healing from my attack. And it did not hurt my perception of the nurses when they commented on what a fine, handsome looking man I am, which is always good for the ego. I realized how special these people — nurses, therapists and social workers — are because of what they do for a living.

Once we were in the car and ready to go, Allison spoke. "Well Greg, if you keep up the good work at home this weekend, you are going to spend a week at home for the holidays."

"Great."

"When we go back Monday, you have two days back before Christmas break. Instead of Tracey, you will have Lou for physiotherapy," Mom said.

My mother never dwelled on the negative thought of having to spend our Christmas at the hospital. It was this hidden motivation, however, that was driving her to work my visits home up to this point. I do not know if she was doing it purposely, being so upbeat and positive about things getting better, but her way of thinking was working.

I did not respond overtly to having a new therapist, but I was nervous. I viewed my therapists as a child in school views his teachers, and I wondered if Lou was going to be strict and demanding. No therapists I had encountered so far were, but that had not sunk in yet.

Once home, my wheelchair was set up and Allison pushed me to our apartment. That was the last time I would use the wheelchair. I could walk slightly, rising and moving like a robot with the assistance of someone beside me. I would also use walls to lean on to keep from falling. Tracey had me walking at her last session. I even walked up stairs cautiously, holding on to the railing so hard that my knuckles turned red. It did not feel like walking because she was holding me and always had her hands on me, twisting and contorting parts of my body that should be moving on their own.

After lunch, Allison set me down on my bed for a rest before supper. "Greg, if you need to go to the washroom, give me or your mom a shout."

"Okay. Thank you."

Allison left and I rested on a double futon mattress without safety bars put up to stop me from falling. I had nowhere to fall, however, as my makeshift bed was directly on the ground. The oscillating fan brought from the hospital was turned on to drown out whatever noise Allison and Mom made, but I could not sleep. I thrashed around in my bed, tossing and turning. Even though I had the fan by my bedside at the hospital, it did not drown out the noise of the television in the lounge or the moans and groans from adjacent rooms. I was used to that and not to extreme quiet. My brain needed time to get used to the silence and was having difficulty doing so.

"Mom!" I yelled, as I had to urinate. Allison came instead. "I need you to help me get up. I have to go to the washroom." She helped me to my bathroom just across the hall and I turned to her and said, "I will try on my own this time."

"Okay. I will be outside the door," she said.

Before I urinated, I glanced at the mirror above the sink and placed my hands on the counter top to lean on. I had seen my reflection before, but this time it bothered me. I looked as thin as my brother, who was very thin. My hair was getting longer but had still not grown over the scar or the area where the intra-cranial pressure-monitoring rod had been inserted.

My beard was coming in, in spots, as the person who used an electric razor to shave me was clearly not a barber. The shave also had to be done quickly because the stimulation was not good for my healing brain. I had not had a clean wet shave since my ordeal because I could not even walk, let alone hold and control a sharp razor to shave. My torso looked like the trunk of a small tree without bark. My T-shirt hung on my shoulders as if it was on a wire hanger. There was no muscle definition. This time, my face showed what was going through my mind. My eyes were squinting and I was shaking my head, which looked like it shook in slow motion.

"What the hell? What the hell?" I whispered softly to myself.

Serious fan

I pushed down my sleep pants and diaper. I was still losing weight, so my pants did not need much assistance to be pushed down and quickly hit the floor. Since the toilet in my bathroom was right next to the sink, I was able to place one hand on the sink countertop to balance myself. I could control my urination and "hold it" for a short period, long enough so I could get to the washroom or have someone help me.

It was nice urinating on my own without Mom or Allison by my side, holding the piss jug as they watched me urinate. Maybe I wanted some of my privacy back, privacy that I had lost in the hospital. However, I was not capable of thinking like that because I was still in a "fog". Maybe it was me getting better and not realizing that pissing on my own was part of the recovery process.

"I am done," I spoke loudly at the door.

"Good. Do you want to sit on the couch and watch some television?" Allison asked.

"Sure."

After I was set on the couch, a football game was turned on the TV. Being hit on the head did not affect the love I had for American football. I did not watch TV in the lounge at the hospital because both the noise and the concentration required in viewing the images exhausted and irritated me. Allison's TV was quite small, and with the volume turned down low, I was able to watch. I was lost as to the playoff picture because I had not followed for a month and a half. I was surprised that the two expansion teams were in the playoffs and happy that my Niners were in the playoffs as well. I had difficulties following the game and had to squint to come close to making out the score or to read statistics flashed on the screen. After twenty-five minutes, I told Mom to turn it off because watching exhausted me.

This was something that changed following my ordeal. Before I was attacked, I cared about how my team was doing and took their win and loss record personally. Now I just enjoyed watching and really did not care about the outcome. I was equally happy whether my team made the playoffs or lost. My love for football, watching sports, and being a serious fan was gone, however. Whether or not the teams I had cheered for previously won or lost did not affect my life, had no meaning in my life's outcome. I do not know why I changed exactly, but perhaps being able to watch sports and urinate on my own was good enough for me.

"Greg, lunch is ready," Mom said. I was helped to the dining room table and noticed Mom sitting at the table with Allison sitting to my right.

"Let's eat," Allison said.

As we "dug" into our lunch and conversed, I realized I was now a serious fan of more important things than professional sports.

Wet thinking

After lunch, I had a couple of hours of attempted sleep. I still was thrashing about.

"Well Greg," Mother spoke as she entered the room, "do you want to have a shower before supper?"

"Yes please."

I was excited to have a shower as I had not had one since the night of my attack. I am not the biggest fan of baths, even though at the hospital the bath was also a Jacuzzi. I stood with one hand on the towel rack and took off my sleep pants. Allison and mom set up the white padded bench to fit the bathtub so that I could sit down. They also placed a rubber bath mat down so I would not slip. Once I sat, I felt the warm water hitting me and was extremely relaxed.

"Greg, just holler when you are finished," Mom said.

"Okay. Thank you."

I sat under the water for about five minutes before concentrating on washing myself. When I began to wash, however, my relaxation turned to frustration. I was having difficulty washing my genitals and my behind because I could not stand. I washed as best I could and sat with the water streaming over me. I was lost in my thoughts.

I started to think about what happened to me that night by linking together all that had been said: from Mom, Allison, and Brian telling me about the attack from behind and being repeatedly hit to the head, to the therapists and social workers telling me about head injury and why my left side was so much weaker than my right and why I could not walk or go to the bathroom on my own. All of these effects were because I had taken such a blow to my head that my brain "rested" for fifteen days. Once I awoke and my brain started to function again, I was like a child and had to relearn everything. But my memory was still intact, making my situation emotionally difficult because I remembered doing such things, like walking, before.

"Greg, are you all right?" Mom asked.

I nodded my head with the warm water from my long hair spraying me like a wet dog. I did not have a haircut because the stimulation and noise would exhaust me.

"Yep, I am finished."

Mother and Allison helped me out and towelled me off. My privacy was not on my mind as I was only capable of thinking of one thing, trying to figure out what had happened to me. Once I was dressed, we gathered at the dining room table for dinner. I was becoming tired from my first full day at home, and I planned to go to bed after I ate.

Mother made pasta with her homemade sauce. As we ate, Mother tore open one of the small envelopes the nurse had given us. Several pills spilled out onto the table, another reminder that something terrible had happened and my life was changed forever.

Another chance

After an enjoyable dinner, I sat on the couch with Mom and Allison.

"So Al, when are you going home for the holidays?" I asked.

"Christmas Eve day."

"You must be excited."

"Yeah, I guess. But I don't want to leave you guys."

"Don't worry. I have Mom."

I felt bad for Allison, because she came out here for a fresh start, like me, and she now had to deal with taking care of a friend who was savagely beaten. I loved her for making the choice of helping Mom and me, for not abandoning me like some of my other friends and even family.

How she acted was unexpected; I was unable to love her before because that person was a roommate who at times I could not stand. Actually, the decision to be roommates was destroying our friendship. This tragedy has somehow brought out a side of her that I had not known. Even the way Allison was acting made me wonder if this was a strange, albeit long, nightmare. She seemed like herself but someone else too, as in a dream.

It was eight-thirty and I needed a good night's sleep, even though I was not looking forward to the tossing, turning, and discomfort I would face getting used to my old bed. I still needed to lie down and try to sleep. As I got ready to sleep, I thought of what I realized today. I still could not believe, and did not want to believe, that something like this had happened to me.

I looked at my unchanged opened closet and then at my arm. I had my hospital band on and suddenly thought that having something physically on me tied me to the situation in which I now found myself. Maybe this tiny band on my wrist that stated my name, hospital name, room number, and date of arrival kept me from waking up from this nightmare. I tore at the band with my right hand, but I could not muster enough strength to tear it away — so I bit at it. I finally broke the band and then started to panic. What if this was real and not a nightmare, and this band brought me luck in how well I was recovering. I grabbed the busted band and tried to put it back on.

I could not, however, and fell back on the hope that it, this little plastic hospital band, kept me from waking up and everything would be back to how it was before now. I fell asleep quickly with the excitement of waking up as my old self, but I still hoped that I had not affected my recovery if I woke up as the same person who went to bed. I hoped for the best.

Same results

I awoke, and as with my thoughts before, I was disappointed. This time, however, I was certain that the nightmare was true. I would have difficulties still grasping this reality at some points, but now I at least would accept that something horrible had happened to me. I would not believe in superstitions anymore either, or put faith in such things as removing a hospital band. Even though I could not physically or mentally give up superstition for the past month and a half, I did so now because, as I told myself, look where it had gotten me.

I used to tap every fingernail from thumb to pinky and back again whenever I hit a fingernail against something. I thought, "Hey my life could be worse," and I believed that by fingernail tapping or by doing any other superstitious routine I had an effect on the outcome of my life. I was wrong.

I was helped through the next day and ate three delicious

meals.

"Greg do you want to watch TV before bed?" Allison asked.

"Sure," I responded.

Allison turned the TV on to *The Simpsons*, the animated sitcom, that I did not forget enjoying. While watching *The Simpsons*, Mother and Allison went into the kitchen to clean up after our supper and chitchatted. As I watched television, Homer, the father, did something that struck me as funny and I began to laugh. It was a loud, sporadic, awkward laugh that seemed different from how I had laughed before. I continued to watch, laughing sporadically, and as I continued to watch, I noticed that the chitchatting and commotion in the kitchen stopped. It then started up again but was quieter.

"Do you still want to watch television?" Mom asked.

"Yes please. There is a new animated sitcom coming up that I would not mind watching."

"Sure," Mom said as she and Allison sat down beside me on the couch.

I turned to them and said, "You got to love *The Simpsons*."

The two nodded in agreement and did not respond. Their eyes were red from crying, but they were quite happy. I continued to watch the cartoons, laughing at parts, with Mom and Allison laughing too. Their laughing was different though. They were laughing with joy from hearing my laughter for the first time.

"Well Greg, do you feel like calling your father before you get ready for bed?" Mom asked.

I was hesitant to respond. I did not want to talk to anybody on the phone because I sounded different and still did not want verification that something like this had happened to me. People commenting on how I was talking and how great I was doing verified it. It did not help that the noise and concentration needed when conversing on the phone drove me nuts. Even though I was becoming agitated, however, I had not spoken to my father for well over seven weeks and missed him and so decided it was time.

"Yes, I would like to."

"Hello," I said.

"Hey Greg. How ya doing?" my father replied, obviously happy to hear me and also curious to hear how I spoke.

"Good. I am walking a bit and I may be coming home for the holidays."

"That's great. You sound fine and all our thoughts are with you back here."

When my father stated, "Back here" I started to feel a heavy weight on my chest, heartache. I realized that this would be my first Christmas in twenty-four years that I would not spend at home with friends and family. Wherever I was, I made a point to be in Sault Ste. Marie (Soo) over the holidays, which was a ritual or superstition I did not mind having and wanted to keep. I did not want to talk anymore.

"Well, got to go to bed Dad. Love you," I said, my father surprised by my sudden need not to talk anymore.

"Love you too. It won't be the same this Christmas without you. Talk to you on Christmas day, Okay."

I handed the phone to Mom. I had trouble breathing and did not respond to my father. I was deeply saddened by the last thing he said. I was panting for breath as I said, "Why did this happen to me?"

I held my hands over my face, as I did not want Allison to see me cry. Allison helped me walk to the couch, and I sat with her beside me. I continued to cry deeply for some time.

"Well Len, talk to you later," Mom said as she hung up the phone and joined Allison and me in the living room.

"I just do not understand," I said, still crying.

I could not comprehend why I was not in the "Soo" this time for the holidays. Deep down I also was saddened that my father was not here now, or when I was in the hospital, for me.

"It's all right, Greg. Neither do we," Mom said.

Allison was right next to me with her arm around me. I looked up and saw her looking at Mom. Both were teary eyed but smiling.

"What is so funny?" I asked angrily.

"Greg, we do not find any of this funny," Allison said.

As when I had laughed, they had tears of joy over my crying. Both joy and sadness were emotions they thought I had lost.

Chapter 10

Walking through the snow

"Allison, after you drop Greg and me off you may take the car and run about. I know you have a lot to do in the next couple of days in order to get ready for the holidays back East."

"Thanks."

We arrived at the hospital, and Mom retrieved my wheelchair. I was placed in it and wheeled to my room. Once I was settled back in, Mom wheeled me to a different room for physiotherapy, where I met Lou, a thin, older man with white hair. He took out a pen and pad of paper and asked me a few questions.

"So what are you doing at the moment with Tracey?"

"Well, I can stand and move slightly."

"Can you walk?"

"Slightly."

Mother then interrupted.

"Tracey has been concentrating on stretching and limbering Greg up. She has been working on his abdominal and back muscles. Greg can walk, but not for long, and is not fluid. His walking is quite robotic."

Lou scribbled in his notepad, and after a few more questions, put his pad away and left, coming back with two wooden canes.

"Okay, stand up."

I looked at Mom and answered with a hesitant, "Okay."

Once standing, Lou placed and held a cane on each side of me.

"Okay Greg, hold onto the canes and walk."

I did walk, but with small slow steps. As I took a step forward with my right, Lou moved my left arm forward with the cane. He did the same when I took a step forward with my left foot, moving my right arm forward. By pushing my arm farther forward, I took bigger steps. Lou acted as my puppeteer, and I did not mind being the puppet. It felt like I was walking for the first time without someone holding me close or contorting me while I moved.

"Okay Greg, I want you to pull the right cane forward when you step with your left. Pull the left cane forward when you step with your right."

I started to pull the canes forward on my own. I would mess up as I did not remember ever concentrating so hard to walk and did not recall moving my arms as much when I walked before. We continued to walk up and down the length of the room. After fifteen minutes of doing so, with Lou narrating me through the steps, he took the canes away.

"Okay Greg, just once, back and forth."

I took a deep breath and proceeded. As I walked, I concentrated on what Lou taught me. I concentrated too much and fouled up several times. I had forgotten that walking was new to me but still did not want to make any mistakes. However, I did walk on my own, albeit slowly, awkwardly and still a bit robotically. Surprisingly, my balance was pretty good, though I did teeter every so often. After my lap of the floor, I sat.

"Very well done, Greg. I will see you tomorrow. Same place, same time?"

"Yes sir. Thank you."

"You're welcome."

Mother brought me the wheelchair, but I did not want to sit in it. I wanted to walk back to my room, and I did, with mom beside me pushing the wheelchair. I looked at the empty wheelchair and smiled. I was very proud of myself for not having learned to manoeuvre that chair. I would not need to now.

Looking too fast

After my occupational session with Paula and lunch, I went to my audio session with Stephanie. I looked out the window and it was snowing.

"Are you sure this is Victoria?" I said to Mom.

"I know. It has been snowing non-stop, and this is the most snowfall Victoria has seen in almost thirty years. Brian said the roads and highways are getting bad. He says for this reason, along with a horrible head cold he has come down with and does not want to give to you, there is a good chance he is not going to make it back for Christmas."

I felt horrible at this news. Mom may miss her first Christmas with Brian out West because of my predicament. What a Christmas for her, I thought. Her family back East, her newlywed husband caught in a snow storm, and the person she was spending her Christmas with, her son, could not take care of himself.

"Sorry Mom."

"For what? Brian means a lot to me, but knowing I still have you makes this the best Christmas yet."

I did not respond. I was extremely touched by what Mom had said and did not know what to say. I wanted to cry, and now that my capacity for emotion had returned, I could; but I held it in with great difficulty, other than brushing away a single tear. Although I had to sit a few times along the way, I walked to audio therapy. My fatigue was a severe problem, as I would tire from the smallest of physical or mental activities.

"Hi Greg," Stephanie said.

"Hi Stephanie, Sharon, Jim."

The blow to my head never affected my short-term

memory and this was evident from the moment I first woke from the coma. I was fortunate at least in this regard.

"Now Greg, do you want to go first?"

"Sure."

"You have been doing well. As in the previous session, the instructor will read the numbers, but now in descending order, and they will be read faster. So, are you ready?"

"Yes."

The "tap" test ended with me only getting four wrong.

"Good Greg. If you can get down to only three wrong, you can move on."

After doing other tests, I went to my group occupational therapy session next door. I enjoyed this session. Stuart, a small man in his eighties who had a stroke, would always make me smile with his sense of humour. Mom and Allison liked sitting in on this session because they thought Stu was the cutest.

After finishing the session, Paula, who was always the first to help me, said, "Greg, instead of coming to therapy tomorrow, I am going to take you downstairs and get your eyesight tested."

I was still having trouble with my left eye. It was getting better, but Paula wanted to see if I did need glasses, and if so, if I would be able to balance and do my tests that involved focusing and reading better. I wanted to find out too.

"Also, after we visit Lou, we will try the pool. How's that?"

"Great."

I was curious and relieved. This meant, given what I was capable of putting together, that I might be well enough to go home for not only the holidays but for good. I was probably getting ahead of myself, but that was easy for me to do that day because going for a swim and getting my eyes checked excited me.

Uncanny resemblance

The night seemed to last forever. Most nights did, because of ailments from my attack, but this one seemed longer than the rest because of my anxiety. The pool, walking with Lou, and mom finding out for sure if I was going home for the holidays were the cause of this.

"Mom, I have to go to the bathroom."

"Okay."

"I will try the patient's bathroom next door."

"Sure," Mom proudly responded.

Mother helped me stand and walked beside me because I was still groggy from the night of tossing and turning. It felt to me like the previous day had officially been my first day of walking, which was still new to me. After I finished and as Mom and I were walking back to my room, I passed John, the social worker at the hospital. He was assigned my file, and I may have met him previously, but I did not remember the encounter.

"Looking good Greg," John said.

"Thanks."

I turned to Mom and said, "Who is that?"

"Oh, John." My mother spoke before he was too far away.

He came back and introduced himself. After our introduction, Mom told me what John did and that he was a major factor in her meetings with the staff about me going home. I became even more excited at my chances now that he had said that I was looking good. Once back in my room, Mother helped me with changing for the day. I now did it on my own for the most part, except for the diaper.

"Greg, let's try underwear today and get you out of those diapers."

"No problem."

I was a very willing participant. Getting out of the diapers

111

was something that I looked forward to from when I first realized I was in them. Wearing them was a reminder that I was very dependent upon assistance for a very basic human need, and knowing I could not even go to the bathroom on my own depressed me and gained my greatest attention. The constant crackling of plastic when I made the slightest movement and the heat they created I could do without too. Once ready, we walked, taking breaks along the way to the therapy room for Lou's session. I sat on the cushioned treatment bed and waited.

"Hi Greg. Let's take a walk," Lou said.

I stood and did my walk, following Lou's directions from the day before the best I could. After my walk across the room and back, I stood in front of Lou.

"Good Greg. Do it a couple of more times."

I did as asked, noticing Lou watching me, his face suggesting that he was deep in thought. I returned and stood once again in front of him.

"Okay Greg, what I would like you to try is to take big steps. With each step, throw your arms to your side as far as you can. Like this." Lou demonstrated to me what he had just explained. "When you step forward with your right, throw your arms to the left. Then when you step forward with your left, throw your arms to the right."

Lou took another walk across the floor to show me what he wanted me to do.

"Okay Greg, your turn."

I started my stiff and awkward attempt cautiously. I was doing it but in slow motion compared to Lou. When I turned back, I looked at Mom. Her legs were crossed, her hand covering her face, and she was shaking. She was laughing. I was disheartened, but now that I was getting my sense of humour back, I was not as disturbed as I would have been previously.

"What are you laughing at?" I asked her.

"Sorry Greg. I can't help it. It's just how you are walking." Mom started shaking again.

"What?" I questioned.

"You look like John Wayne."

Lou chuckled to himself. I found it funny and jokingly mouthed the words "That hurt" to Mom.

"Okay Greg, I want you to now walk the same way but to try and turn your head and look to the side as you take a step."

"Okay."

I did as asked, stumbling at first and forgetting to turn my head a few times. The problem of only being able to concentrate on one thing at a time was still present. After a few back-and-forths, I came to a halt and stood at attention in front of Lou. Mom was sitting to his right, still trying not to laugh. I then said to him with frustration, "I do not remember ever walking like this before my head injury."

"You just walked with as much exaggeration as possible. With your injury, you will forget the exaggeration and remember enough to walk normally, not like John Wayne."

It made sense. By this John Wayne way of walking, I would remember to take bigger steps and move my arms to the left and to the right when taking steps. It also got me used to turning my head to look around.

"Thank you," I said to Lou, "for teaching me this."

"You're very welcome. You have done enough for today, but do the 'John Wayne' over the holidays."

"Yes sir. Merry Christmas."

"To you too."

He turned and said good-bye to Mom as she got up, and along with the lone ranger, left.

Strutting

I was lying down in my room waiting for my pool therapy with Paula. I did not know what to expect. I could swim before but not too well.

"Well Greg, I will bring another change of clothes so you are fresh after you swim."

"Thanks Mom."

We walked to the pool. I did not know there was one because the curtains in the windows were always drawn around it.

"Okay Greg," Mom said. "Go ahead in."

I walked into the men's change room and sat on a wooden bench. A lady who introduced herself as Pam handed me swim trunks.

"Thank you."

"You're welcome. Can you change on your own?"

"I can try."

"I will be just around the corner if you need me. Call me when you are ready."

"Okay."

I took off my shoes and clothes and was naked. I did not notice the metal curtain rod around the space where I changed. Neither did I realize that the change room door was being held open by a stop. There I was, nude and saying hi to people of all ages and of both sexes. I was getting strange looks for my politeness and wondered why I was receiving them. I looked to my right and saw a large curtain, and then it hit me.

"Oops," I said to myself as I pulled the curtain around my space. Once I established a little privacy, I finally put on my swim trunks and called for Pam.

"The floor is slippery," she said as she guided me out of the change room and to a small pool. The smell of chlorine was quite strong.

"Hello Greg."

"Hi Paula." Paula was already in the pool, and Pam led me to the railing of the stairs that went into the pool.

"Take your time," Paula said.

I slowly walked down the stairs, resting both feet on the same stair before taking another. The water was very warm, and my pool experience felt extremely comfortable once I was in Paula's outstretched arms.

"Okay Greg, let's take a walk."

The pool's water came up to my nipples and was of uniform depth other than a step down for the deep end.

"What is so good about the pool is that, if you make a mistake, the water breaks your fall," Paula said.

After a couple of walking laps from poolside to poolside, we went into metal parallel bars that were located across the middle of the pool. Paula attached more bars under the water, which kept me between them.

"Now Greg, grab onto each bar and allow your feet to float up behind you."

I leaned forward and my feet started to rise. The only problem was that I could not keep my upper body afloat. I held the bars tightly, and Paula noticed the problem I was having.

"That is enough," Paula said.

"But why can't I float?" I questioned in a defeatist tone.

"Well Greg, you have so much muscle mass in your chest that you need strength to hold it up, which is something that you do not have much of at the moment."

I looked to Mom, who was at poolside watching, and grinned. It was good for my ego to hear such a thing. I left the pool and went into the change room and sat while Pam helped shower me. I still was smiling, proud of myself. I still had it.

Chapter 11

Set sights

After the pool therapy, Mom and I returned to my room. Allison was back at our apartment getting ready to go home, back East, to be with her family for the holidays. That was something I had planned to do as well, but even if the tenth of November did not take place, I would never have been able to afford the plane ticket back.

"Well Greg, I am meeting John, your social worker, your therapists and doctor to see if you can go home for the holidays."

My previous nervousness about going to my apartment for the holidays had lessened with how I was recovering. My nervousness was still there, however, because the fact that things were not going my way before this happened to me was one of my greatest sources of anxiety. Along with the excitement of getting better and going home for Christmas came the thoughts of failure and what I was going to do once I got discharged. I did not want to have to do what I was doing before. Scrubbing toilets and walking home during the wee hours was why I was here.

The pride I got from my father made me mop floors and take a job that was not meant for me. I did not want anyone's help. I wanted all those I left behind back East to think I was making it. Maybe most of them did think I was making it, however. Maybe leaving unnoticed helped.

Mom left for her meeting and I stayed awake, staring at the clock and ceiling. I then looked at all the get-well cards taped to the walls in my room. They know, I thought. They know I was failing and almost died failing. Why did I care what the people from my past, and for that matter the people of my present, thought? I was becoming angry with myself.

How could I let this happen? How could I let not only the tenth happen, but how could I let everything happen to me that brought me to this point? Why didn't those jackasses finish me? I don't want to go through this again: the pressure of fulfilling people's expectations, my expectations. Lying in here was not working towards where I wanted to be when I turned twenty-five years old.

"Great news, Greg. You're going home for a week, and we only have to come here on Monday for your therapy and to check up on how you are doing at home. If things go well, you may be going home for good soon."

"Great," I said with no emotion.

"Is everything all right, Greg?" Mom questioned.

"Yep. Let's get these eyes checked with Paula."

"Okay."

I remembered Paula's appointment, which was a good sign of recovery memory-wise. Remembering also was why I was becoming angry, however.

"Okay Greg, set your chin on the rest and your forehead on the strap. Look straight ahead and tell me where the dots are located."

Paula, Mom, and I were in a different part of the hospital, the basement. In the basement is a cafeteria for visitors as well as patients to use. There also were more extended-care rooms, and where I was located was a place for out-therapy. Therapy I would hopefully recover enough to receive. Out-therapy meant that I would come from home for the therapy session, and the session would be the only reason I was at the hospital.

The room the three of us were in contained computers and the machine I was at that tested my eyesight. The lights were turned off and I stared straight ahead. Paula then started to push buttons, which resulted in small dots of light being revealed in front of me, either straight ahead or to the left or right.

"Ready Greg." Paula said.

She had been pushing the buttons for a while. It was not that I misunderstood the instructions, but my mind was not concentrating on the test but on the new surroundings I was in. My lack of concentration had only showed once in a while previously. I was aware of it when it happened, and as I sat in the basement to have my eyes checked, I made a note to myself of the need to improve. Having unaffected memory allowed me to do so.

"Oops, sorry," I replied as I now focused on the test.

"Left bottom, top, right top and bottom, middle, left middle, right top."

The test continued for another five minutes, with ten second breaks as Paula took notes. We then stopped.

"Very good Greg. Your eyesight is fine, and at the moment it looks like you will not need the assistance of glasses."

"Great," I responded.

Mom and I got up and thanked Paula for her help. We walked through the out-therapy area, and I turned and looked back as we went out the door. I stumbled, a bit, doing so, but I now could finally fully see where I wanted to be.

True Meaning

Mom and I returned to my room. I was going home at four o'clock. It was Christmas Eve, but it did not feel like it. I had to pack up what few things I had.

"Greg, they are renovating this part of the hospital, including your room, so can you give me a hand with taking down these cards?" Just as Mom finished speaking, I flopped onto my bed.

"Oh Ma, I'm weak. I do have a head injury you know." I laughed into my pillow. This was the first time I used my problem as an excuse, a blatant one.

"All right." Mom chuckled back.

We packed everything up and got my medication from the nurses' station. After we picked up my meds, I passed Bob in the hallway and wished him a merry Christmas. We slowly continued our walk, and I noticed the residents and patients in wheelchairs were alone. Some of them looked blankly out the windows at the snowflakes falling to the ground. Some Christmas: a hospital-cooked turkey dinner, and if they were lucky, a loved one would be there for them.

I remembered back to when I walked home from work and passed the brick with gold capital letters: the Gorge Road Hospital sign. I did not see the hospital itself because it was quite a distance from the road. The hospital is also downhill and trees line the S-shaped lane that leads to the front door, adding to its hidden aspect. Maybe the hospital was designed this way so it could be forgotten, as a majority of the inhabitants are forgotten by society and more sadly by family. I was guilty of not being aware of this place and those who lived here.

"Merry Christmas," a younger wheelchair-bound man said as well as his condition could allow him.

"Merry Christmas," I said back.

The automatic doors slid open as I wiped a tear from my cheek. I will not forget ever again.

Mom and I were lucky just to drive the two blocks to my apartment. The rare snowfall Victoria was receiving was not easing up. We carefully trudged through the accumulating snow to the front entrance of my building, and Mother allowed me to open the glass door. I had some difficulty turning the key and opening the door, proving that I was still very weak.

We took the stairs not only for my benefit but Mom's as well. She is claustrophobic and avoids elevators because of her phobia. I lived on the fourth floor, which was not too bad, but when I was at the General Hospital I was on the sixth. The tiring, scary, repetitive walks she had to endure up the enclosed stairwell I could not imagine. I never want her to have to take that type of walk again, or any more elevator rides for that matter. I was starting to think of my mortality and that of those around me, which was another sign of getting better as I was analyzing such profound subjects. These subjects did not help me in being happy for the holidays or as a person generally, however.

I opened my apartment door. This was the first time I had done so in a month and a half. Allison was there to greet me with a hug.

"I am leaving in an hour so I am going to give you your Christmas gift," Allison said as the tightness of her hug lessened.

"You did not have to."

Her helping me was the greatest gift anyone ever gave me. Thankfully Mom had gone and purchased Allison a sweater and candles for our material gifts for her. Mom handed them to me to give to her when she gave me mine. We exchanged our presents and sat on the couch beside one another to open them. After ripping the paper and tape off my gift, I opened the box to a pair of "funky" corduroy pants, a pair of jockey shorts, and a compact disc.

"Thank you," I said.

"Thank you," she said in return, looking at Mom as well because she knew I obviously did not do the shopping.

We stood up and hugged again. Allison then went to her room to finish preparing for her trip back East.

"I am going to miss her," I said to Mom.

"I know. Me too."

Allison came back into the living room carrying her luggage. "Well Greg, I will be back on the second, so have a great Christmas and New Year."

We then hugged, and as I held her I spoke into her ear.

"Thank you for all that you have done for me. I am going to miss you."

"I am going to miss you too. Love you."

"I love you."

This was the first time I remembered saying such powerful words to Allison. I might have in my messed up state over the prior six weeks, but this time I understood the meaning behind those three words. After our hug and Mom saying goodbye and hugging Allison, she left. I felt great sadness; a part of me had just left. I was falling in love.

Alone

Mom and I sat around my dining room table eating a wonderfully prepared ham dinner, just the two of us. I looked at the empty chairs around the table. It was Christmas Eve without siblings, parents, grandparents and relatives. When my parents separated when I was twelve, Christmas always seemed like work, keeping both sides happy. Two turkey dinners, one with my father's side and one with my mother's side that I had to endure. This routine turned Christmas into more of a hardship than a celebration. I now missed that routine and realized how special it was.

Even though my parents were apart, I still had Christmas dinner with them and their new family members. Having something suddenly taken away from you that had been there your whole life puts a new perspective on what you thought was a hardship or a repetitive, sometimes annoying event. I took Christmas for granted, for even though there were ill feelings between my parents and their respective families, I still had the holidays with them before.

This perspective was my new focus: not to take anything I gained back from my injury for granted, from times with my family, laughing, crying, walking, talking, writing, to even taking a crap and wiping my ass on my own. I prayed that I would have a chance to fully have back all this to cherish for the rest of my life.

"Would you like some more ham or scalloped potatoes Greg?" Mom asked.

"No thank you. Could I have a piece of fruit though for desert?"

"Why don't you have a chocolate bar with some eggnog?"

"Okay," I answered hesitantly.

Whenever I asked for a piece of fruit, Mom would respond that I should have a chocolate bar and eggnog instead. I wanted to get back to my healthy eating habits but forgot I was now under one hundred and twenty pounds. I was not upset obliging Mom's suggestion and ate a chocolate bar and drank a large glass of eggnog whenever I was given the opportunity. We both giggled as I downed my unhealthy dessert. I looked at Mom after slowly drinking the last of my eggnog. She smiled, pointing out my eggnog moustache, and I wiped it away. I had Mom with me for Christmas and this was enough.

I was lying in bed awaiting sleep, but something new was happening. Whenever there was extreme quiet and I was concentrating on sleeping, my head pulsated. Along with this pulsation came a ringing in my ears. It would go away, or maybe it didn't and I would finally fall asleep. Before I did fall asleep this Christmas Eve, however, the phone rang. Not its usual ring but a double ring, which meant someone was "buzzing" up to be let in the security entrance of the building.

"Who is that?" I shouted.

"It is Brian. He made it!" my mother answered back with excitement. I was so happy for Mom and myself. Brian would help take away the loneliness of this Christmas caused by a horrible occurrence. I did not get up to greet Brian because I could not. Before I hollered hi and Merry Christmas to him, my bedroom door opened and our two family cats scurried in.

Mom brought them with her when she moved out West.

"Puny, Bitsy," I said as the two purred around me. These are ironic names for the two as both enjoy eating and being lazy and therefore are quite large. But hey, they are house cats.

"Hi Greg. How is it going?" Brian asked.

"Not too bad. I'm happy you made it."

"Me too. The roads are horrible with this strange winter weather. I don't want to get too close. I am just starting to get over a chest cold, so have a good night. Do you want the cats out of your room?"

"No, it's all right. Just leave the door open, thanks. Good night and Merry Christmas Brian."

"You too."

I was so happy to have Brian and my two lazy, purring pals with me. It was not a big Christmas, but it would certainly do. I was thrilled just to have another.

Chapter 12

First Christmas

I awoke at quarter to eight in the morning. My body clock was set to the hospital schedule, and I awoke at this time every morning.

"Merry Christmas Greg," Mom said as she opened the door to my room. Mom also knew of my wake up schedule because she was there for a majority of those mornings.

"Merry Christmas, Mom."

"I am going to help you up and give you your gifts."

Once in the living room, Mom set her presents at my feet. I was saddened that I did not have any for her or Brian or any other family member. I began to cry, which was now very easy to do. Similar to every emotion I was gaining back, when it revealed itself for the first time, it was extreme. I had to teach my brain when to use an emotion and to what degree. I had met others at the hospital with this problem, laughing or crying at suspect times. I, along with them, was emotionally labile.

"It is all right, Greg." Mom did not ask why I was crying. She knew. She knew how I wanted to buy nice gifts for my family, showing I was successful and had made it.

A sweater, socks, underwear and a pair of jeans were my nice gifts.

"Why don't you try on your jeans?" Mom said.

"Sure."

Whenever the chance came to dress myself on my own, I did. Putting on pants was a way to practice my balance. I staggered and lost my balance a few times but finally got into my new jeans. They fit well but were a bit loose. I undid the zipper and looked at the small tag. Thirty-inch waist. I used to wear thirty-four and even thirty-six inch waist pants. I always wanted to be thin, but not this thin. I walked into the living room and modeled my new gift.

"Ohh, those fit good, Greg."

"Thanks Mom."

I sat on the couch and asked, "Is it too early for eggnog, Mom?"

"No."

"Could I have some?"

"Sure."

The way my body was burning calories, why not take advantage of this?

"And are there any chocolate bars left?"

Opposite

After lunch, I crawled into my bed for an afternoon nap before Mom's Christmas dinner. I did not sleep and thought of what was going on back East. I thought of Allison and my family; their Christmas was also different from previous years. I was sure that the conversation around my father's dinner table was quiet and somber, the same with Allison's, my brother and sisters' in Windsor. I wondered what was said and was even curious.

I never wanted to go through what they went through with me, for me, because of me. I always feared something happening to a family member or someone close in my life, and now this feeling was magnified. I also pondered how I would react. Not like my father. Where was he anyway?

I did not recall him at the hospital like my other family members, and why did he not come out here for Christmas? I had tossed and turned with my thoughts for a couple of hours when Mom entered my room.

"Greg, it is almost four, so do you want to get up and we

will have supper?"

"Yep."

I got up with Mom's assistance and we went to the dining room table. While Mom prepared dinner, I asked Brian, "Why isn't my father here?"

"Well Greg, your father, when he came here to see you at the hospital, did not handle it well."

"How come?"

Before Brian answered Mom interrupted. "Greg, your father has a lot of problems himself. He was, and still is, overwhelmed by your ordeal. He probably would have had a breakdown or heart attack if he remained here any longer. It was best for you, and especially for himself, to leave when he did."

My father owned and recently lost his restaurant in the "Soo" owing to the depressed economic state of my hometown and was having difficulty getting by.

I did not respond and asked if supper was almost ready. It was, and Mom began to set the many wonderful entrees, the turkey with all the trimmings, on the table. Once the table was set with our feast, we joined hands and Brian said grace.

"Heavenly father, thank you for this special day and the birth of your Son, our Saviour. Bless this food to our body and continue to give guidance to those who are working on Greg's recovery. Please continue doing so, as we know you are. Watch over our family and friends and help them deal with the hardship created by Greg's misfortune. We pray in your precious Son's name, amen."

Mom and I replied with amen.

I looked at Mom and Brian as they began to serve our meal. How Mom and Brian reacted is how I would react if someone I loved were severely injured. Which is easy for me to say, however, as I have yet to take such a test. I do not ever want to.

Snowfall

After my second night at home for a week-long holiday away from the hospital, Mom, Brain and I decided to go for a Boxing Day walk. The snow had accumulated to about two feet. The strange occurrence of such weather created havoc as Victoria was snowed in. The city had one snowplow, and it alone could not clean up a city of Victoria's size. The three of us bundled up for our trek, and we all took the stairs, and not just because of Mom's claustrophobia. I, as well as my support, took the "nothing ventured nothing gained" approach to my daily life. However, I would not take on stairs by myself, and safety was our utmost concern. I always kept my fall at the hospital in mind.

When we got outside, Mom stood in front of us and began to speak. "Okay Greg, we shall go slowly due to the treacherous conditions, and when you feel tired, we will sit down." There were several benches scattered through the condo complex's landscape. We planned to go around the building my apartment was in.

"It is very slippery here in the parking lot Greg, so be careful. Brian, get right beside him," Mom directed.

She was even more concerned about the walk than I was because she had read information on head injury and knew that there is a high incidence of subsequent head injuries due to a survivor's greater risk of falls. My balance was good, but not great, as I experienced moments of unsteadiness.

"Okay guys, let's go."

Just after Mom stated that, she turned and took one step and both her feet, along with the rest of her, became air born. She slipped on the icy conditions she had warned me about and landed on her bottom. Thankfully, she did not hit her head. She shook the fall off and stood, turning around to face Brian and me. There was silence, but once I knew that Mom was fine, that was broken by my different, gasping attempt at laughter. I sounded like a walrus and was joined by giggling from Brian and then Mom.

"See what I mean," Mom chuckled.

After Mom's actual proof of what could happen, we began our walk. The day was beautiful as large snowflakes fell on us. Mom walked in front of me, and Brian in back. We did not do much talking as we made it to the halfway point of going around the building. There was a bench that was snow-covered and I stopped, wiping it off to sit.

"I have to sit for a minute or so," I said to Mom and Brian.

I was not only tired from the walk but thinking of how to walk: left foot forward with right arm, right foot forward with left arm. I said those commands to myself with every step.

"Shoot, is it going to take this much effort to walk, not just physically but mentally?" I said disheartened.

"It will take time for your brain to remember it naturally, because it needs time to learn," Mom said.

The various steps necessary for walking were now part of my conscious thinking, and hopefully with time that information would enter my sub-conscious mind, and walking would involve no in-depth thought.

"I guess you're right," I replied.

As I sat, I looked all around at the scenery, especially at the evergreen trees whose branches were bent from drifts of snow on top of them. I listened to the wind whistling and water gurgling from the Gorge Waterway that was about fifteen feet away. I remembered recognizing BC's beauty before, but not like this. I did not realize how special it was to take it all in, let alone being able to do so. I had a new perspective on my life and what it could be.

"Shall we continue on Greg?" Brain asked.

"Let's go," I said.

"Left foot, right arm, right foot, left arm," I said to myself.

I focused on my walking and hoped it would come naturally like Mom said, along with appreciating all that was around me.

Trailblazers

"My car is buried and the roads are as well," Brian stated.

It had snowed off and on since our walk, and with the lack of snow removal capability in Victoria, the situation was becoming dangerous. However, I had to go back to the hospital to let them know how my week was going and to do a physiotherapy and occupational therapy session. I would not spend the night as it was the thirtieth. The therapists and other health care professionals who took part in my rehabilitation did not work on New Year's Eve and New Year's Day.

"I think Greg and I can make it up the hospital by walking," Mom said.

"It is uphill and a pretty tricky walk with the conditions caused by the snow," Brain replied.

"We can make it," I said.

My confidence was growing and I wanted to increase it by taking on such a challenge. Mom was thrilled with my growing confidence and we started to dress for our walk.

"Be careful. Love you," Brian said, hugging Mom and me before we closed the door.

When we got outside, the sidewalks were not cleared, but a path was packed down from previous walkers.

"Well Greg, let's do it."

"Lead the way," I responded.

The walk was very difficult because if you went off the path your foot would fall even deeper into the snow. This caused you to fall to one side, and to regain your balance and equal footing, you had to lift your leg out of the fresh hole and get back on even terms with your other. Mom and I had to do this over a dozen times as we continued to walk. It was comical as we laughed at each other falling to one side and then the other. We finally made it to the hospital.

"We will go to the nurses' station and see what is going on," Mom said.

The hospital's activity on this snowy day was similar to nighttimes in that all was very, very quiet. We made it to the nurses' station and asked for Lou, my physiotherapist.

"Sorry, Greg. Because of the weather, your therapists did not make it in. One therapist did make it in by cross-country skiing. How was Greg's week at home?" she asked my mother.

"Excellent. He is really improving. So much so that we walked up here."

"In this? Good for you Greg."

"Thanks."

"One thing we can do is take some blood. Greg we want to see if we can cut back on you anti-seizure medication."

"Sure."

I was needle-phobic, although I probably had a lot of experience with them since my arrival into hospitals almost two months ago, but I was willing. To ease up on Dylantin, my anti-seizure medication, would be great. The medication was horrible for my teeth and gums, as one of the side effects of the medication is gingivitis. I took off my coat and sat down. Being aware of the needle this time sparked my nervousness, which was tripled by my head injury and having to relearn and cope with such an emotion.

"Ready Greg?" the nurse asked.

"Yep."

She inserted the needle after tying a tourniquet around my bicep.

"I am having troubled finding the vein."

She reinserted the needle four times and said, "We're going to have to switch arms. Sorry, Greg."

"No problem," I said shakily. She inserted the needle in my other arm and found the vein on the first attempt. I guess it took four attempts to finally realize I had another arm.

"Good stuff, Greg. Thanks," the nurse said when she finished.

"You're welcome," I said as best I could without letting my anger seep into my voice.

"Well Greg, shall we get going," Mom said.

"Sure."

"Are you too tired?"

"No, I will be all right." We bundled up and began our walk. I looked ahead to our path. It would be easier this time because home was downhill from here.

Chapter 13

No turning back

Allison arrived back from her holidays the day after New Year's. My New Year's celebration consisted of my mother hooting and hollering on my balcony. Mom, Brian and I called this year, 1997, the year for me, the year for recovery. It was Friday, with one more weekend before I returned to the hospital, hopefully for just a couple of weeks. The way I was feeling and recovering made me expect to return for two weeks; however, I knew of the danger of creating expectations that could not be realized from my past.

Allison had a busy traveling day, a five-hour flight, an hour bus ride, an hour and a half ferry ride, and finally a forty-five minute drive. Head injury or not, such a venture would tire anyone. After conversing for close to an hour about her family and trip back East, Allison lay on the couch in a semi-fetal position caused in part by me sitting at her feet. We watched television, occasionally throwing out banter. We were both getting exhausted.

Mom and Brian had gone out for dinner, to be followed by coffee at a trendy café. With the two of them gone, the evening was reminiscent of the old times, the days prior to my assault. But unlike those times, something new was evident. Love instead of hate was in the air, and what would take place that night revealed that I was not the only one affected by this.

"I think I am going to go to bed," I said.

"If you want you can lay in behind me."

"Sure," I answered in a surprised tone as Allison moved towards the edge of the couch.

I had not had a girl in my personal space for about three years, and now I did with Allison, a girl I never dreamed or imagined having this close to me. Even in my brain-injured state I was able to understand that I might not have an opportunity like this again owing to my uncertain future. I did not know how well I was going to recover and felt Allison was my only chance at love.

As I was coming out of my haze, I started to see some of the unloved people at the hospital, those who were unloved because of no fault of their own. Being disabled in the shallow world of today meant your best chance was with someone like yourself. Such common ground is hard to find.

I squeezed in behind her and we laid spoon style, my pelvis pressed against her behind, my chest against her back, with my right arm across her waist. My perverse way of thinking returned, as I was able to slide my hand under her sweater and rested it on her defined stomach. She did not respond to this action, so I started to ponder if I should follow my perverse thoughts.

As I pondered, I began snapping the waistband of her underwear ever so gently. After about the third time, I began to lower my hand, but before I could any further, Allison spoke: "No. You better not."

I removed my hand and sat up. An abrupt end was what I needed because I then thought of the repercussions of carrying on with my attempt at intimacy.

"You're right." Before I could expand on why this was the case, Allison sat up and leaned into me. We were face to face and began to kiss passionately. I gripped the back of her head with my unaffected right hand and continued on. I did not lose my ability to kiss, as the passion did not subside.

"Let's go to your room," Allison said softly as she exhaled.

We got up and slowly went to my room holding hands. I would have gone faster, but slow was all I was capable of. As I shut the door behind us, I hoped the old times would not return now and I would think of her as I had before.

What went on in my room between us changed our relationship. We now had more than a friendship. We had companionship. This companionship had officially begun on the tenth of November. Allison had quit her job with no other reason but to be with me. This was something only a wife or companion would do. This was one of the major reasons why I created intimacy between us, why I decided to do what I did on the couch. At first I was turned back, but then she let me in, into a closeness I thought I would never have a chance at again.

I did not share the same view as Allison did regarding our intimacy. I have not spoken to her in almost eight years now and probably will not ever again. I could write about what happened to us and have, as therapy, but will not include those events as part of my journey, my life, my ID. I will not reminisce about the nastiness that our relationship evolved into.

As I recovered, I changed and Allison changed as well, but she went back to being the same person I knew before my assault. The new me, however, created a greater distance between us. I was accepting of our strange, and at times frustrating, cohabitation before my assault, but I was not so accepting afterwards. Creating intimacy was the gasoline needed to ignite an always burning fire rather than the water I thought could extinguish a smouldering past. This is my view and mine only, however, and Allison may view things quite differently.

Although I try to forget our attempt at companionship, I do not ignore the girl who was there for me, the near stranger who was my angel for my nearest to death experience. This is how I now choose to remember Allison and how I want to remember her.

Close by

I looked to the right at my alarm clock on the floor beside my bed, which read seven thirty. I had to get up to be ready by 8.30 to leave for the hospital. Before I got up on my own, I looked to my left, where Allison slept.

What a week of holidays I had. Allison and I had become more than friends, at least I had assumed so, and I had become more independent, especially in regards to my mobility. I was able to rise, with the support of a wall, on my own. I was proud of this, as I did not have to yell for someone's help.

My progress was remarkable, physically and mentally, even though the latter was difficult for me to measure. Having to recall all the steps involved in every task I did, from walking and dressing to brushing my teeth, was my measuring stick.

After my shower and once dressed, I got myself a bowl of cereal with milk. I sat and ate while Mom scurried around my apartment. I had remembered where Allison and I stored our cereal and where we kept our bowls and utensils. The smallest of events that seemed so unattainable weeks ago, like preparing a simple breakfast, were coming back with no thought.

"So how long do you think I have until I can come back home for good?" I asked.

"I don't know. It is up to the rehab team, and more importantly, it depends on your rate of recovery," Mom answered with a smirk caused by the possibility of my discharge coming sooner rather than later.

I was not saddened by having to return to the hospital; I knew I was receiving the best rehabilitation as an in-patient. I also missed my friends, especially Bob. I was starting to realize how special and important those around me were. My family, friends: old and new, were there for me. I had an excellent support system, which was to key in my miraculous, continuing recovery. I was wary of a plateau in my recovery but felt I could climb higher as those with me cheered me on.

"Well Greg, let's go," Mom said.

I ate my last spoonful of cereal and brought my bowl and spoon to the kitchen, rinsing them out and setting them in the sink. Mom finished packing a tote bag with my usual attire: track pants, sweaters, T-shirts, swim trunks, socks, and underwear, along with my toiletries. Brian folded up my wheelchair, not asking if I wanted to use it. I felt the same way as Brian's action implied. I would never use the wheelchair again, except maybe if I needed a place to sit.

The four of us drove back to the hospital and a smile came across my face. This time it was not forced and difficult to make. I was happy that I had survived a terrible ordeal and that I might even come out of it a better person.

Odds & ends

Allison and I walked to my first session back holding hands. We passed John, my social worker. John thought we were boyfriend and girlfriend when I first arrived and was surprised we were not. He gave a quick smile with a nod to the two of us and continued on. Just by this simple gesture I could sense he was not enthusiastic about my new situation. I had enough issues to deal with without taking on the additional burden of a relationship.

My first session was with Dee. She set up canes in the form of X's, four of them that spanned three quarters of the hallway.

"Greg, what I want you to do is walk backwards over each X, placing your foot in each area dissected by the canes. Try not to touch them and go very slowly."

I was perplexed but understood the instructions. How this activity applied to my daily life, when and how I would use this movement, I could not comprehend. I succeeded through the "X marks the spot" exercise. Dee did not have to instruct me to go slow because a turtle would have gone faster.

"Excellent, Greg. Next I want you to bounce this ball as you do it."

"Seriously?" I questioned.

"Yep."

"Okay."

Dee handed me a rubber ball the size of a grapefruit. I dribbled it and lost control of the ball a few times. Having to divide my attention between dribbling the ball, avoiding the canes as I concentrated on walking backwards, and listening to Dee and Allison complimenting my success, made this very frustrating and difficult. I did make it through the course, however.

"Okay Greg, one more time," Dee said.

"Shit," I humorously gasped to myself, but I made it through slightly faster this time.

"All done. I will see you later on in the week."

"Thanks." Allison and I then walked to my OT session with Paula.

" Hey Greg. How were your holidays and your week at home?" Paula asked.

"Great. I feel awesome," I said, glancing momentarily at Allison.

"Good. What I thought we would do is set up a time for you to cook a lunch, later this week, in our kitchen. Come with me and we will check out the kitchen." We followed Paula to the kitchen and she gave me a tour. She showed me the on/off dials for each stovetop element and for the oven. She also showed me where all the dishes, utensils, and pots and pans were located. We then sat at the table in the kitchen area. I remembered the kitchen and sitting at this table for my attempt at baking ginger snaps. Not a fun memory to have, but I did remember

"Is there a dish you would like to prepare?" Paula asked.

"Pasta and sauce with garlic bread. Is it all right if I cook enough for us plus Mom?"

"Sure. What ingredients should I order for our lunch?"

"Plain tomato sauce, a can large enough for four servings. Some penne macaroni, parmesan cheese, a large green pepper, fresh white mushrooms, a cooking onion, and garlic bread, the kind that comes in tin foil that you put in the oven for fifteen to twenty minutes."

Paula nodded her head as she wrote down my order. She seemed impressed with my planning.

"And to drink?"

"Ice water will do."

"Great, Greg. On Wednesday, we will put this together. So see you at noon."

"No problem," I said.

Allison and I then walked to physiotherapy. All my sessions after the holidays were strange in comparison to those before my week off. I went from a bizarre activity with Dee to something done everyday with Paula. I wondered what physio would focus on. I and my therapies were both changing rapidly.

By chance

"Greg, today you are going to ride the stationary bike for our time together," Lou told me.

"Sure."

I got on and began to pedal, which felt awkward at first, but after a few times around, however, that awkwardness lessened. I was thinking that if I had ridden a bike that night, I would have not gone through any of this. Hindsight is twenty-twenty, and I was starting to exhaust myself with such vision.

The "What if?" questions were entering my mindset. While I was pedaling, an older, Asian man sat on the treatment bed to my left.

"Hello," he said.

"Hello," I replied back. Being early into my bike ride, I was not winded yet and able to talk.

"So, how did you end up in here?" he asked.

This would be the first time I would answer this question on my own. I told him what I had managed to piece together.

"I was walking home from work in the wee hours, about four thirty in the morning I think, when I was struck from behind and assaulted. I do not remember anything from that night and spent fifteen days in a coma, with an additional fifteen at Victoria General. I have been here, at the Gorge, for about a month." This explanation sounded good to me, and I was proud to be able to explain in my own words what had happened to me.

"I gather you received a brain injury?" he added.

"Yes." Before I had a chance to ask him about his story, or even his name, a nurse entered the gym and said, "You are in the wrong room sir." The two then exited.

I had ridden the bike for about twenty minutes when Lou interrupted. "Okay Greg. That is it for today. How do you feel?"

"Fine."

"No dizziness."

"No."

"Okay then. Tracey is back tomorrow so you will see her."

"Thanks a lot, Lou. You have been so helpful," I said, and I shook his hand.

"All the best Greg."

I went back to my room for lunch. When I got there, the stranger I had talked to in physio was conversing with my mother.

"Hi Greg. This is Patrick. He was telling me about your talk and suggested you see his son, who is a neuro-chiropractor, for a couple of sessions."

"Sure," I said. I was receptive to trying anything that could lead to greater improvement. I shook Patrick's hand and he gave me a business card with his son's name and office number on the back. I turned it over to the front and the card revealed my new acquaintance was the head of the medical program at a well-known Canadian university. His son, to whom he had referred me, was a world-renowned chiropractor specializing in brain injury. Just from our meeting and quick conversation, I received an appointment for treatment sessions that would have been expensive and therefore unattainable.

"Thank you," I said.

"You're welcome. When you leave here, call my son and mention who you are and he will arrange an appointment for you."

"Again, thank you so much."

"My pleasure."

I would not see Patrick again, but he, like everyone else who had entered my life at that time, helped me in my recovery. I started to notice such encounters were not by chance, but for a reason.

Whiffs

After lunch, I was lying in my new room and looking at the ceiling. I was moved to a different room that was located closer to the exit of the hospital. The room was isolated from the others and very quiet. The last time I was this deep in thought was the night before my assault. That evening, I was cursing out God and asking for a sign. If this was my sign, it was more than I bargained for. I was very tired and needed to rest, but my mind was racing with what was happening and with many questions.

As my brain healed and came out of its fog, I began to question the "what ifs" that led up to that night. This thinking was spurred on even more from my bicycle ride and meeting Patrick. What if Patrick went to the right room in the first place? Each question led to a waterfall of several more, to trying to find an answer for each. I thought of "what ifs" as far back as my childhood and up to the present, like what if Tracey did not take holidays and I did not meet Lou? Would I be progressing as well as I was with my walking?

What if my parents did not separate? What if Mom never met Brian? Maybe if my parents could have tried harder at their marriage, then perhaps my mother would not have met Brain and the option of moving out West would have been eliminated for me. What if I did not fail university? What if I did not move out West? Maybe I could have looked harder in Windsor for employment and even went back to school. It was not like I was excelling out West, even though I did not have the opportunity to do so.

What if Allison did not mention the batteries running low on her bike light? I would have ridden her bike. What if I did not try to fix mine, thereby damaging the brakes? The answer to that last question made the one about Allison void, for I would have ridden mine, passing by whoever did this to me

What if I had bought that knife my best friend Mando and I were looking at a couple of weeks before my assault? My perpetrators would have probably used it on me and I would not be here. What if the Niners football team did not play the early game on Sunday? I would have stayed and had my coffee, instead of getting it to go. What if I did not apply for a BC health card, which I got on November third, a week before my assault? I could not answer all my what ifs, and the ones I could answer did not yield pleasant answers and led to that night. That night resulted in the hardest "what if" of them all.

What if I jumped from the bridge and was not attacked? I started to cry. I did not want to think of the repercussions of the answer to this one. I turned my head and reached with my arm for the blinds on my window, separating them with my fingers. I looked out into the hospital's courtyard. There sat a lady in a power wheelchair with a loved one sitting beside her, wiping her mouth. He was talking to her and she would groan a response. I released the blinds and closed my tear-filled eyes: what if?

Chapter 14

One of many

My therapists were all impressed with my continued recovery, especially with the week off. I did not fall back in terms of my progress without therapy, but rather, I even improved. Mom and Allison attended another meeting with all of those involved in my rehabilitation. The two came back to my room, ecstatic.

"Greg, you are being discharged this Friday, January tenth," Mom said.

"Awesome," I replied.

"I have to do some running around, so once again, congrats on going home. See you later. Bye," Allison said

"Bye."

It was two months since my assault and I was going home. Going home so quickly made what happened to me even more unbelievable. It also scared me. What was I to do after this? Go back to mopping floors, or maybe talk to the department store that I was going to work for prior to my assault? I was told that I would have to learn to live with the symptoms and deficits caused by my brain injury, but owing to my fortunate recovery, I did not think it would be a problem and ignored the fact that some of the deficits were permanent.

I was excited to live my life by my own schedule, but I did not know what my schedule would be and what my time would encompass. I knew it would consist of outpatient therapy and coming back to the Gorge Road Hospital almost daily. What about the other twenty-two hours that made up a day? At least half of them would be used for sleeping/resting, and the other eleven were for leisure and work. I knew I had to find employment to support myself. The government was there for me during my worst times allowing me to have expense free health care, but sadly this was not a sign of things to come.

Receiving my head injury via an assault was not an insurable accident. I would hear from others, professionals and survivors, that I would have been much better off to jump in a car right after my assault and hit a pole so I would have insurance to fall back on for financial assistance. Having to deal with the bureaucracy, that my mother dealt with and soon me, in proving my disability would turn out to be extremely difficult and exhausting.

"Greg, are you all right?" Mom asked.

"Yeah, I am looking forward to going home. I guess I am just tired."

"I know. You have one more session in OT and then you are done for the day. Would you like anything special for supper?"

Mom was ready to take down my order and go home and prepare my dinner as she usually did, but I responded by saying, "I will have the hospital food. I think I would like to be alone this evening. Why don't you and Brian go out for dinner? I know he is heading back to the mainland tomorrow."

"Are you sure?" Mom was confused by my lack of enthusiasm, especially at the news that I'd be going home.

"Yeah, I am sure. Thanks. Better get to my next session."

"Okay, see you tomorrow."

Mom may have taken my request personally, but she was set at ease when, before she left, I said, "Thank you for everything, Mom. Love you."

"You're welcome. Anything for my son."

"Can you tell Allison I will see her tomorrow as well?"

"Sure. Bye Greg"

"Bye Ma."

I watched Mom as she walked down the hallway and

exited the hospital. Trying to gain back my independence was my biggest feat to conquer, and telling those around me not to help as much would hurt them more than me. I hoped that Allison would react the same way as Mom had reacted.

Pressure cooker

It was Wednesday, "hump" day as it is referred to in the working world, and I was becoming anxious. John, my social worker, told me that it could be years before I worked again. He stated that I needed the present time to concentrate on rest and relaxation. This was difficult for me to accept because "r and r" did not pay for food, shelter, and the other costs that went with a normal life. My life in the hospital focused on one thing: my recovery. I did not have the pressures of an adult living on your own. The "picket fence" theory that hampered me before my assault was creeping back into my thoughts. I still had trouble accepting that something life altering had happened to me with the miraculous recovery I had.

Meeting with John that morning helped me, however. He put direction into the next few months, and this quelled my concerns for the time being. I was not happy with the direction my life was taking, pre-head injury, but I did live on my own without help or support. Did I want my previous life back? No, but having the opportunity to succeed without a disability I would definitely take in preference to a life of being supported by someone else.

After an hour of talking with John, I had my session with Paula. Today was the day I was going to prepare lunch for her, Mom, and Allison. I did not view it as an assessment of my abilities, and this was good, but rather as preparing a meal for others. I remembered learning in my human resources courses in college that a person is less productive and more likely to make mistakes if someone is watching over them. I felt this way in my physiotherapy sessions with Tracey and other therapy sessions, but with Paula I felt comfortable. I walked into the kitchen, and Paula was there as well as Deb.

"Hey, Greg. How are you?" Paula said.

"Good."

"You remember Deb."

"Yes, ginger snaps." The three of us chuckled.

"Deb is going to help you out, and I will be ducking in and out once in a while to see how things are going," Paula said.

"No problem," I responded.

Paula stepped out and Deb spoke: "Okay Greg, make your meal as if you were at home, and if you have any questions, I am here. I will intervene if you are having any troubles or there are safety issues."

"Thanks."

I was a bit dumbfounded by the safety issue comment and analyzed my own actions as I began to prepare my meal. I was probably unsafe in preparing my meals before the attack and never realized it, and now I would probably taint the assessment with being aware of it.

I washed the vegetables for my sauce and placed them on the cutting board. I took out a large knife from the drawer, holding it blade down as I walked with it to the counter. I used my right hand to chop as I held the onion, green pepper, and mushrooms with my left. I did notice a difference in the ability of my stabilizing left hand and knew to place it far from the knife as I chopped. I knew losing a digit would not impress. I then took out a large, deep pan and poured two tablespoons of olive oil into it. I turned the element to mid-range heat, and as it warmed, filled a pot with water for my pasta. I put the pot on the back element and turned it to high heat. I added salt and a teaspoon of oil to the water.

"Greg, why did you turn the heat to high?" Deb asked.

"Because there is lots of water, and by the time it begins to boil, my sauce will be ready."

"Okay," Deb responded as she scribbled into her notepad.

After answering Deb, I placed my chopped mushrooms and green pepper into the pan. I then took out my garlic bread in foil and a can of sauce from a grocery bag and placed them on the counter. I read the baking directions for the garlic bread on the back of the foil. After placing the onions in the pan, I remembered that onions are quick to cook and thus added them last. I then turned on the oven to 375 degrees to preheat for the bread. I stirred my vegetables and then sat down across from Deb at the table, asking her, "How is it going?"

She smiled and responded with, "Good, and you?"

"All right."

"Any questions or problems?" she said.

"No, not yet."

I turned down the heat for my vegetables and added my sauce, stirring everything together. I then added the pasta to the boiling water. I put out enough dishes and utensils for five, occasionally stirring my sauce and pasta. I then put the garlic bread in the oven.

"I would say in about ten minutes everything will be ready. Where can I find a strainer for the pasta?"

"The cupboard under the sink."

"Thanks."

I placed the strainer in the sink. I then turned the elements off and grabbed the pot of boiling water with pasta. Before I lifted, however, Deb intervened.

"Greg, let me show you the best way to get this pot to the sink."

Deb took out a dishtowel and placed it, folded, on the counter beside the stovetop. She then lifted the pot and set it on top of the folded towel, sliding the pot to the sink. I donned oven mitts and emptied it into the strainer. I was impressed with Deb's strategy. My way of getting the hot pot of water to the sink was the only "blip" in preparing a dinner for five, and I was happy, as was Deb, with how my meal prep went.

Mom, Allison, and Paula then arrived.

"Okay everybody, we will do this buffet style. Grab a plate and help yourself," I said as I cut the bread.

I watched as everyone dished up their meal and began to eat. For that split moment it felt like nothing terrible had happened to me and I could accomplish anything.

First, not last

Mom purchased assorted boxes of chocolates, small date-books, and numerous cards, which I signed, for me to hand out to the wonderful people who were essential for where I was at in my recovery. These tokens of appreciation were not only for my caregivers but for my wonderful new friends as well.

"I will meet you guys at the car. Is it out front?" I said to Mom and Allison.

"Yep, I got everything but your tote bag," Mom said.

"I will grab it. Thanks," I said.

I wanted to say my goodbyes on my own, and these two wonderful women understood. I wanted to show that I had gained my independence back and tackling such a difficult event on my own showed this. It also displayed for those I was saying farewell to had a vital part in the fact that I was walking out of the hospital on my own.

First, I went to Paula, my occupational therapist, and gave her a date book along with a card. I knew Paula would use it as she taught me the importance of a day planner and that it would be helpful for me to use one, memory problem or not. I told her basically what I had written in the card, but without the grammatical errors,

"Thank you Paula. I really appreciate your help and the extra effort you gave me in my recovery."

"My pleasure, Greg. I will see you, I am sure, while you attend out-therapy here. Take care."

"Is it all right if I give you a hug?" I asked

"Definitely."

I squeezed Paula as hard as I could, which I am sure felt like a light hug to her, but to me it was strong.

I gave little gifts with cards and said good-bye to Tracey, Dee, Deb, Stephanie, John, and Lou. I would see John at least once every two weeks for the next few months but still wanted to give thanks to him. After I gave a big box of chocolates to the nurses' station, I had to say my toughest good byes.

I walked the halls searching for my dear friends and came across Sharon first.

"Bye Sharon."

I bent over and hugged her and then gave her a box of chocolates and card. I felt guilty for leaving her behind. We entered the hospital roughly at the same time, but this is all we had in common. My recovery had gone a different direction than hers. Sharon did not get worse but did not get better either. But her ailment left her with much greater problems to deal with than mine. I was so sad for her.

I then went to Stuart's room. He was in bed but awake and lying on his back. I set some chocolates and card on his bedside table.

"Bye Stuart, take care eh."

I offered him my hand and he took it with his unaffected hand, setting his flaccid other hand on top.

"You take care. And say goodbye to your mother and Allison for me," he stated as he shook my hand.

"I will. Bye."

Mom and Allison would be touched by Stu's good-bye, as they were his biggest fans. I then went on looking for Bob, my dearest friend, to whom I had opened up first and who always told me to smile and that things would get better, even though they were not for him. I approached Bob, bent over and gave him a hug. As I held him, I said, "I love you, buddy. I will be back to see you. So take care." My voice was starting to crack with emotion.

"You too, Greg. Be careful and know that I love you and He loves you," Bob pointed up.

I gave him his gifts and returned to my room. I grabbed my tote bag and started to walk down the long hallway that I was wheeled down so many times before. I turned back and saw Bob tucking his card beside him and opening his chocolates on his lap. I then focused forward, and similar to when I first entered this hospital, was straight-faced. This time it was my overwhelming happiness cancelling out by my overwhelming sadness that left me expressionless.

I also had great worries. I felt safe on this side of life. I had met and lived with the most caring and loving people, men and women who should have been angry at what life had dealt them. Instead, they had reacted in the exact opposite manner. As the sliding doors opened and I stepped into the cold air, I hoped the freedom I had fought so hard for and the world I so badly wanted to return to would be the same as they had been before.

Chapter 15

The reason why

It was just seven months after my assault that I decided to do some volunteer work with other head injury survivors. I went to the indoor pool facility not really knowing what to expect. I talked to Stacey, the coordinator assigned to Vincent. She set up such appointments for him owing to his inability to do so from the cognitive deficits caused by his head injury. Stacey also kept "tabs" on Vincent's ability to handle all his activities of daily life. More importantly she would provide what was needed for him if a new environment were required because adaptation to a changed lifestyle was not possible

Stacey gave me a brief background on Vincent. He suffered an open head injury from a motor vehicle accident and spent months in a coma. I gave Stacey the okay to give Vincent the lowdown on myself; I thought by having head injury in common we would be able to have a better understanding of one another and bond easier as friends.

The automatic door opened as I stepped on the rubber mat. I walked into the Diamond Pool building very anxious, as I had never served as a helper or aide to someone who was incapable of living a normal life due to injury or illness. I assumed Vincent to be functional as he lived on his own. I thought this because of my own experience. I was ignorant of the varied outcomes from head injury and Vincent was about to show me this.

I stepped through the door and looked to the right to the table and chairs in front of the canteen counter. Stacey told me that Vincent is older, bald and small in stature and that he used a walker to assist him in ambulating. I continued to scan the eating area and my attention focused on a small silver walker and the seat it was in front of. In it sat Vincent looking down. I approached him and introduced myself

"Vincent."

He turned his head and looked up at me.

"I'm Greg."

"Hhhiii, Greg."

Vincent had more of a stammering than a stuttering impediment. Stacey had told me of this and to continue to repeat what he said until he was in agreement with me. Standing in front of and above Vincent I noticed the large scar on his scalp. The scar was the shape of a question mark beginning at the center of his head and ending with his left eye acting as the period.

"Are you ready to go for a swim?"

Vincent did not respond but stood up. When he did he teetered away from me and with my surprisingly fast reflexes I was able to grab him and prevent him from falling. It is also fortunate that Vincent is well below five feet tall and under one hundred and thirty pounds, making my save more attainable. After the near fall he began his walk towards the change room. I walked beside him and would hold his walker so it would not move. Just the short distance from the canteen to change room I could see the great difficulty he had.

Vincent would push his walker forward and not be able to keep up with its momentum. His legs would fall behind him as his upper body went forward with the walker. His body was almost parallel to the ground, when I held the walker still he then became upright. Conquering the stairs not just getting to them was our next feat. I grabbed Vincent's walker with one hand and steadied him with my other. He grabbed the railing and we took one step at a time. We succeeded and once to the top Vincent pointed out the empty wheelchair to our right.

"At least we are not in one of those." He spoke with little difficulty.

I was speechless and in awe. This little man who could barely walk or move for that matter, ten feet was happy not to be dependent of a wheelchair. His life would be easier if he used one but he preferred this way, I would too. Pride and to be who you are before your head injury is the strongest motivation even if it meant endangering yourself. Vincent was this way and I was and would be if I did not recover as well as I did.

We made it into the change room and Vincent sat on one of the many wood benches situated in front of the rows of lockers. At this point I had no clue as to what to do. Stacey never got into the dressing and undressing of Vincent and this was definitely new to me. I "winged" it as best I could, using my personal hospital experience and how Mom and Allison changed me.

"Okay Vincent we will take your coat and shirt off first while you are sitting."

He did so with no assistance from me. I had to remind myself he lived on his own and was fully dressed when he arrived at the pool, meaning he did the getting dressed process that morning The struggle he must endure in just getting dressed made my heart heavy. From that point on I made the decision to do as much as l could for Vincent giving him a three hour, once a week break from the struggles he endured. I intervened to help with the removal of his shoes, socks, and pants and donning of swim trunks.

"Okay Vincent. I'm going to help you the rest of the way. You don't mind?"

He shook his head no. I asked because of that pride in being independent factor.

"Stand up bud and you can rest your hands on my shoulders."

I squatted so he could do so and once stood up undid his belt and zipper and pulled his pants down to his knees.

"You can sit down now."

I took his shoes and socks off and finished removing his pants. After putting his swim trunks on and undressing and putting mine on I placed our shoes and clothing in a locker. Once I placed our belongings in the locker Vincent asked for his change purse from his pants. I gave it to him and he removed a quarter. He then gave it to me pointing at the locker. The locker was coin operated. Once the quarter was placed into the locker it released a key with safety pin when turned and our belongings were then locked and safe.

"I will get the next one." And the next one and the next one.

The decision to give Vincent a break from hardships that able people do not have would also include a break financially. I would pay for everything from locker to snack afterwards while waiting for his bus. He was not going to unzip that change purse in my presence anymore. Times are tough for me as a head injury survivor but not as tough as Vincent's. Bob's lessons were rubbing off on me.

We were now ready for our swim. To say I was not making a mess in my pants thinking about our walk through the slippery shower area and onto the pool deck would be a large lie. We began our treacherous walk with me holding his walker firmly, taking small steps together. I too was not fleet of foot in regards to balance and coordination from my head injury. Once through the showers we entered the pool area. My own recovery was put to the test, as what I saw was the most stimulation I encountered since my assault. The Olympic size pool and hundreds of people swimming, diving, and taking classes and me being there with my impaired acquaintance made me take several deep breaths.

I had to gather myself. I was not even told what class we were in. I did an irresponsible thing next, climbing into the pool with Vincent, in the deep end using the metal bar with steps as my support. I stood there one hand on the bar the other around Vincent's waist. Thank God for his size. I was immersed in water with my "head injured" buddy attached to my hip. I almost began to weep, as I did not know what to do next.

"Do you need a hand?" a rotund, older lady asked.

"Yes. We are in the aquatics class at ten o'clock."

"It's down near the shallow end. Would you like some life preserver belts?"

"Definitely, thank you so very much."

We climbed out of the pool and the saviour of a lady returned with two lift belts. I placed one around Vincent's waist and one around mine. I was very much at ease wearing the belts.

I relearned how to swim after my head injury but was no Mark Spitz. We descended to the shallow end where a gathering of older people was forming in the pool.

"Hi Vincent," the attractive instructor said.

I assumed she was the instructor because of her age, not being in the pool and standing in front of the class.

"Hi I'm Cindy."

"I'm Greg."

"So you're going to be with Vincent for the next little while?"

"Yes, at least till the new year."

"It is so nice to see a son be there for his father."

"Ah, I'm not Vincent's son, I'm a volunteer."

"Oh I'm sorry."

"That's all right, maybe apologize to Vincent." We both chuckled with Vincent sporting a grin.

I stood behind Vincent with my hands on the life belt around his waist. I would remove them and let him attempt some of the exercises taught by Cindy. I remembered Paula and my self in the pool doing therapy and how that the water was there to break my fall if I needed it. The class lasted an hour and we approached the forty-five minute mark and Vincent began to tire.

"Okay people, let's go to the wading pool and sit and do our last few exercises."

We all got out of the pool and made our way to the smaller warmer pool, sitting around the rectangular, two and a half feet deep area. I positioned myself squatting like a baseball back catcher in front of Vincent to prevent him from falling over or teetering to one side. As he sat on the step his eyes began to roll back.

"Are you all right?" I questioned.

He moved his head up and down slightly indicating a yes and tried keeping up with Cindy's instruction. After another minute his eyes began to roll back again.

"Okay bud we've done enough for today."

With me saying this he attempted to follow through with the exercises once more, he did not want to leave and finish the whole hour like everyone else. I turned and looked at Cindy and mouthed the words that we were leaving. She agreed, brushing away a tear. She was shaken by Vincent's great effort, as was I, but I kept it together.

We made it back to the locker room. I was now very confident in walking with Vincent. Before sitting down he stated he needed to go to the washroom. I transferred him to the toilet and shut the stall door behind him. I stood just outside waiting for him to finish. I looked to my right arid caught the stare of a man who was at a urinal finishing his business. We both nodded a greeting and I noticed he was visibly upset holding back his tears.

"Yeah, ah, is that Vincent Mills?"

"Yes it is."

"Damn, he used to work on my car. He restored and repaired bodywork on all types of vehicles and the best in town at it. He was so friendly and such a great guy."

With that the stranger left not being able to continue to hold back his emotions. What an eye opening experience I was having. I had to hold back my emotions and just gaining this emotion back caused me to choke them back literally.

"Are you done Vincent?"

I barely got the question out with all that I witnessed in the past ten minutes or so. "YYyes."

We made our way to our locker and did the thirty minute process of getting showered and dressed. While we showered I let out my tears allowing them to be camouflaged by the streams of water thrown upon us. I did not want him to see me cry.

I saw so many things, actions/behaviours, in Vincent that I did as well but recovered from more fully than him. He must have checked for his change purse twenty times with me checking for my wallet twice. He was in a coma twelve times as long as me, I am not a doctor but understood that the longer you are unconscious lessens your chances of recovery. Vincent being twice my age was also a factor.

We made it to the canteen and l sat Vincent at one of the tables. We had about an hour till his transportation arrived. Stacey said I could leave right after the class but I was not going to let Vincent be alone. I was now sure he spent a majority of his time alone because we talked earlier about our families. He asked me if I had a wife and kids. I was able to decipher from his answer that his wife left him when he was comatose and that he has not had contact with her since. I did not ask about children because that was enough for him to bear.

I bought a hot dog and two cokes, putting the condiments he liked on the dog. Buying him the hot dog instead of for me meant I would have to sacrifice my dinner tonight but this was worth it. When I sat his snack down he reached for his change purse.

"Don't even think about it. You can get the next one."

He was okay with this. He would not, however, get the next one. Even though it was cruel, I would use any memory problem Vincent had, as I would say, "You got the last one." We did not talk much while he ate his hot dog and we drank our cokes. We did not need to because we were both content. Vincent made me realize that the simple task of having lunch was a special event

"Well we can sit outside and wait for your bus. It is such a beautiful day."

We made our way outside sitting on a bench while we waited. The sun felt so warm as it beat down on us. Our silence was broken by Vincent's clearly spoken question.

"Greg why did you bounce back?"

My heart was now in my shoes while I thought of how to answer such a question.

"I don't know Vincent, I don't know."

I looked up to the clear blue sky where a few large white puffy clouds made their way across.

"Thank you, God, thank you." I said to myself

I helped Vincent stand and begin his walk towards the parked bus. I looked at our full reflection on the glass wall of the building. I had my arm on Vincent's back, making sure he did not fall. I bounced back to be there for Vincent and others in need. I was so grateful God picked me.

"Jesus is the image of the invisible God" Colossians 1:15

The Blanket

All of us become cold, unloved, unwanted.
We look for warmth under covers,
through fire,
and from those close by,
but we still are cold.

We need a blanket whose fabric
is made of this and more.
A part of that fabric must come from inside
to wrap around the soul, the spirit,
destroying the coldness from flesh
and warming it with love.
We all have this blanket.
It is there for everyone to use.

This blanket is created with life
by God
through Jesus Christ.

Epilogue

(Questions Answered)

15 chapters, a chapter for each day I spent in a coma.

It has been quite the journey.

Did I get the sign I asked for when I looked up to the ceiling over nine years ago? Definitely yes.

Was it God?

No, but it was He who pulled me through and gave me direction from such a horrific event. He placed angels in my life to pull me through. These angels not only assisted in my rehabilitation but they transformed me into who I am, a God fearing individual who helps others going through the same tribulation.

I now have been working, in some capacity, in the rehabilitation of head injury survivors since seven months after my injury. I went back to school, graduated with honours as an assistant in rehabilitation, and have been employed in the field of neuro-rehabilitation for over four years. I also speak and give presentations on my story and head injury awareness.

Am I grateful?

Yes, God has made it so that I am grateful for what happened to me. Not only through my work, through what I can do. I have perspective now and do things I thought not possible before November tenth. I have written this book and have nearly completed a second, which entails my struggles and perseverance after I was discharged from the rehabilitation hospital. I also have run two marathons for the simply reason that I can. Having everything taken away made me realize how special such things, as writing and running, are. And those are just two of numerous functions and abilities I have greater appreciation for.

Would I forgive those who assaulted me?

Yes, but I will not forget. I celebrate November tenth as a second birthday. My life's direction came from my assault, and greatest of all my eternal life as I now believe Christ is my saviour. I suffered but He suffered for all and for my sin. It took my miniscule suffering in comparison to His, to realize this.

I will end my story with a question only God knows the answer to:

Why not Greg?

Index

109, 110, 112, 114, 116, 117,
118, 129, 134, 143, 146, 149,
155
Tom, 40, 41
Tonja, 14, 16, 22, 40, 79, 80
Toronto Rehabilitation
Institute, ix, x
torso, 67, 76, 98
Tourism, 16
Tracey, 54, 55, 57, 62, 69, 70,
74, 92, 93, 94, 96, 97, 107,
139, 141, 145, 149
trauma, 25, 30, 50, 54
traumatic brain injury, vii
true survivor, ix
Twenty-three days of my life,
56

U

University of Victoria, 15

V

Vancouver, 14, 15, 69
Victoria General Hospital, 23
Victoria Police, 22, 23
Victoria., 19, 30, 31
Vincent, 151, 152, 153, 154,
155, 156, 157, 158

W

Wayne, 113
wheelchair, 46, 47, 49, 51, 52,
55, 56, 60, 61, 63, 64, 67, 69,
72, 75, 76, 81, 84, 87, 90, 91,
92, 96, 97, 107, 108, 119, 136,
142, 152, 153
Windsor, Ontario, 12

165

Ordering this Book

*Wholesale inquiries for this book should be directed to any of the following:

Europe: Gardners Books Ltd
+44 1323 521777: email: custcare@gardners.com
 USA: Ingram Book Company (ordering)
+1 800 937 8000 website: www.ingrambookgroup.com

*Online Retail Distribution: All leading online retailers including
www.amazon.co.uk, www.amazon.com, and
www.barnesandnoble.com

*Shop Retail: Ask any good bookshop or contact our office:
http//:www.adonis-abbey.com
Phone: +44 (0) 2077 938893